1 Introduction

In spite of substantial and persistent economic slack, the United States experienced only a mild disinflation during the "Great Recession" and the subsequent slow recovery. Inflation, measured by the core personal consumption expenditure price index, averaged 2 percent between 2003 and 2007 and only declined to an average annual rate of about 1.5 percent over the following six years, a period that saw the deepest contraction in economic activity since the Great Depression. The absence of a prolonged and potentially devastating deflationary episode has cast doubt on the empirical relevance of the Phillips curve—a central tenet of many macroeconomic models—which posits that a high level of resource underutilization should cause inflation to fall over time (see, for example, Hall, 2011; King and Watson, 2012).

This so-called deflation puzzle occurred against the backdrop of extraordinary turmoil that swept through financial markets in 2008, which motivates us to analyze these two phenomena within a unified framework. Specifically, we seek to understand inflation dynamics during the financial crisis through the lens of customer-markets theory, while dispensing with the assumption of frictionless financial markets. As shown by the seminal work of Phelps and Winter (1970) and Bils (1989), pricing decisions in customer markets—markets in which a customer base is "sticky" and thus an important determinant of firms' assets and profitability—are a form of investment that builds the future customer base.[1] In the presence of financial frictions, however, firms experiencing a liquidity squeeze accompanying a fall in demand may find it optimal to maintain—or even increase—their prices and sacrifice future sales in order to boost current cashflows, a price-setting behavior that can help rationalize the countercyclical behavior of markups; see Gottfries (1991) and Chevalier and Scharfstein (1996) for early theoretical expositions of these ideas.

In this paper, we explore this idea along two dimensions. First, we demonstrate the empirical relevance of this phenomenon for the Great Recession by constructing a novel micro-level data set, which contains *good-level* prices underlying the U.S. Producer Price Index (PPI), merged with the respondent firms' income and balance sheet data from Compustat.[2] Though containing only a subset of respondent firms, dynamics of producer prices implied by our data closely match the contours of aggregate PPI inflation during the 2005–12 period. The main advantage of these data is that we can analyze directly how differences in firms' internal liquidity positions—and other factors—affected their price-setting behavior during the recent financial crisis.

The key, novel finding that emerges from this analysis is that firms with limited internal liquidity significantly *increased* their prices in 2008, a period characterized by the widespread disruptions in credit markets and a sharp contraction in output. Their liquidity unconstrained counterparts, by contrast, slashed prices during this period, a move consistent with the standard pricing models and the New Keynesian paradigm. In addition to being highly persistent, these differences in the price-setting behavior between liquidity constrained and unconstrained firms were concentrated

---

[1]The stickiness of the customer base may reflect a variety of microeconomic mechanisms: costly switching Klemperer (1987); costly search Hall (2008); or idiosyncratic preferences Bronnenberg et al. (2012).

[2]Standard & Poor's Financial Services LLC ("S&P"), Compustat.

in nondurable goods manufacturing, a sector where "experience" goods are more prevalent and where firms' pricing decisions are thus more likely influenced by customer retention and acquisition considerations, the hallmark features of customer-markets theories. Thus, our empirical evidence strongly supports the notion that in periods of financial distress, the interaction of customer markets with financial frictions can significantly attenuate the downward pressure on prices resulting from a drop in output.[3]

Second, to explore theoretically the macroeconomic consequences of financial frictions in customer markets, we build a general equilibrium model, in which monopolistically competitive firms face costly price adjustment, while setting prices to actively manage current versus future expected demand. We do so in the context of the "deep habits" framework formulated by Ravn et al. (2006), which we augment with a tractable model of financial market frictions, featuring costly external equity finance. As in Gourio and Rudanko (2011), customer base in our model is an asset—isomorphic to the firm's financial capital—and the presence of financial distortions affects the incentive of firms to invest into customer base via price reductions.

Relative to a setup with frictionless financial markets, our model implies a significant attenuation of the response of prices to contractionary demand and adverse financial shocks. The key mechanism driving this result is the interaction of financial frictions with customer markets. Faced with a sticky customer base and costly external finance, firms are confronted with a tradeoff between current profits and the longer-run consideration of their market share. Maintaining its market share requires a firm to post low prices. However, a firm can be forced to deviate from this strategy if an adverse shock induces a sufficiently severe deterioration in its internal liquidity position. In that case, a firm will find it optimal to raise prices—and sacrifice its market share—in order to avoid costly external financing, a pricing behavior that resembles a myopic optimization of current profits.

Extending our theoretical framework to allow for differences in financial conditions across firms, we further show that firms with weak balance sheets raise prices relative to firms with strong balance sheets in response to adverse demand or financial shocks. Because firms with strong balance sheets are better positioned to reduce prices and "steal" market share from their financially constrained competitors, heterogeneity in financial conditions leads to a further deterioration in the liquidity position of financially constrained firms, which amplifies the overall contraction in output.[4]

These theoretical results accord well with our empirical evidence, which shows that in 2008, firms facing a dearth of internal liquidity actually increased prices, while their financially stronger counterparts lowered prices. Financial distortions also play a key role in the cyclical behavior of

---

[3]Empirical evidence from narrowly defined industries and earlier time periods supporting this hypothesis is provided by Chevalier and Scharfstein (1996), Asplund et al. (2005), and Lundin et al. (2009). Montero and Urtasun (2014) document a significant increase in price-cost margins during the 2007–11 period for a broad cross-section of Spanish firms; the increase in markups during this period was especially pronounced for firms facing tight credit conditions and for firms operating in industries with a low degree of product market competition. Kimura (2013) presents evidence that the pervasiveness of liquidity constraints among Japanese firms damped deflationary pressures arising from significant slack in the post-bubble Japanese economy of the 1990s.

[4]In the standard financial accelerator model (see Bernanke et al., 1999), by contrast, financial distortions reduce input demand but do not directly affect the firms' pricing decisions. In such environments, alleviating the severity of financial frictions for a subset of firms *reduces* the degree of amplification obtained through the financial accelerator.

markups: In the model with financial frictions, markups remain elevated for quite some time after the initial impact of an adverse demand (or financial) shock; in the case of frictionless financial markets, by contrast, the countercyclical dynamics of markups are significantly attenuated, as the initial increase in markups is offset by low future markups. Thus, the interaction of customer markets and financial frictions can account for the countercyclical nature of markups as well as for the stabilization of inflation at positive rates against the backdrop of significant and long-lasting economic slack.

The puzzling behavior of inflation during the Great Recession and its aftermath has led to a proliferation of research aimed at reconciling the observed inflation dynamics with the canonical Phillips curve-type relationships linking the rate of change in prices to the level of economic activity. Among the most prominent explanations for the missing-deflation puzzle are the "anchored expectations" hypothesis and explanations emphasizing alternative measures of economic slack (Ball and Mazumder, 2011; Gordon, 2013; Krueger et al., 2014).[5] Although this work provides considerable support for the combination of the anchored expectations hypothesis and alternative measures of labor market slack, the case of missing deflation appears far from settled.

In a recent paper, for example, Coibon and Gorodnichenko (2015) point out that explanations involving the short-term unemployment rate as a measure of economic slack imply—in addition to missing disinflation in prices—an absence of deflationary pressures in wages, a pattern that is conspicuously missing from the data. They also present evidence that survey-based measures of household expectations were not fully anchored during this period and were very sensitive to swings in oil prices. Households' inflation expectations, which they argue are a better proxy for firms' inflation expectations than professional forecasts, rose sharply between 2009 and 2011 in response to the surge in energy prices stemming from the resumption of growth in emerging market economies. This fortuitous increase in inflation expectations prevented the downward adjustment of prices and can account for the missing deflation, according to their results.

At the same time, some recent research argues that, in fact, there is no missing deflation. Del Negro et al. (2015), for instance, show that a standard New Keynesian model augmented with the financial accelerator mechanism can successfully replicate the broad contours of inflation during the 2008–12 period, without relying on large exogenous markup shocks. In their model, the drop in output and the associated fall in marginal costs generate substantial deflationary pressures in late 2008 and early 2009. However, the monetary policy feedback rule implies a strongly stimulative policy going forward, which raises expected future marginal costs and thus helps stabilize current inflation. Their results also rely heavily on the estimated degree of price stickiness, which is notably higher than that implied by microeconometric evidence (see Bils and Klenow, 2004; Nakamura and Steinsson, 2008).

---

[5]The first idea stipulates that the Federal Reserve's credibility has led economic agents to discount inflation outcomes outside the narrow range bracketing the Federal Open Market Committee's 2-percent inflation target, thus preventing actual inflation from falling much below that level through standard expectational effects. The second idea argues that the relevant measure of economic slack is not the overall unemployment rate, but rather the short-term unemployment rate, a measure that increased less sharply than the overall unemployment rate during the Great Recession.

Within the context of New Keynesian models, Christiano et al. (2015) also draw attention to the impact of financial frictions on inflation dynamics during the Great Recession. They show that the combination of a risky working capital constraint and a decline in total factor productivity can quantitatively explain the behavior of inflation after 2008 with an empirically plausible degree of price stickiness. In their model, the jump in credit spreads in late 2008 induces a sharp rise in the cost of working capital, which significantly increases firms' marginal costs—the "cost channel" documented empirically by Barth and Ramey (2001). At the same time, the economy is hit by a series of exogenous negative technology shocks, which also boost firms' marginal costs. These two factors counteract the emergence of significant deflationary pressures and deliver only modest disinflation in the face of a significant contraction in output.

Although financial market frictions play a key role in the work of Del Negro et al. (2015) and Christiano et al. (2015), neither of these papers seeks to account for the differences in the actual pricing behavior of firms in different financial positions during the Great Recession. And while the cost channel also arises naturally in the context of our model, it is not the primary mechanism through which financial frictions influence inflation dynamics during the crisis. Rather, our approach offers two distinct contributions to this literature. First, it provides new empirical evidence on how firms in different internal liquidity positions actually change their prices during a financial crisis. Second, it provides a link between these new micro facts and the macroeconomy by developing a tractable general equilibrium model, in which the strategic interaction of firms operating in customer markets and facing imperfect capital markets can in periods of widespread financial distress lead to economic outcomes characterized by a severe and persistent contraction in economic activity that is accompanied by only mild disinflation.

2 Empirical Evidence

2.1 Data Sources and Methods

To document how changes in the condition of firms' balance sheets affected their pricing behavior during the Great Recession, we construct a novel data set using micro-level data from two sources: (1) *good-level* (confidential) producer price data underlying the PPI published by the Bureau of Labor Statistics (BLS); and (2) *firm-level* income and balance sheet data from Compustat. As emphasized by Nakamura and Steinsson (2008) and Goldberg and Hellerstein (2009), the good-level PPI data are transactions-based prices that are representative of the entire U.S. production sector and are consistently sampled, both across production units and time. Goods produced by each firm are uniquely identified, according to their "price-determining" characteristics such as the type of buyer, the type of market transaction, the method of shipment, the size and units of shipment, the freight type, and the day of the month of the transaction.

The granularity of these data allows us to overcome limitations inherent in working with macro-level price series because we can aggregate good-specific inflation rates to the firm level and thus preserve the cross-sectional heterogeneity of firms' pricing decisions. In combination with the firm-level balance sheet data, we can then analyze directly how differences in financial conditions between firms translate into difference in their pricing behavior during the financial crisis. Our empirical approach thus represents an important advance over any analysis that employs aggregate price indexes—even if narrowly defined—to study this question because price dynamics at both the product and firm levels are subject to large idiosyncratic shocks, especially in periods of economic and financial turmoil (see Bils and Klenow, 2004; Nakamura and Steinsson, 2008; Gopinath and Itskhoki, 2011).

We focus on producer—rather than consumer—prices because the PPI data yield a much broader match with the universe of publicly traded U.S. companies covered by Compustat. Economic considerations also point to studying producer prices because they directly capture the price response of production units to changes in the underlying economic and financial conditions.[6] The PPI data also exclude prices of imported goods, which are an important part of consumer prices, but for which data on financial conditions of the underlying production units are not readily available.

We use the algorithm developed by Schoenle (2010) to match the names of firms in the PPI and Compustat data sets. After applying the algorithm to the two data sets over the period from January 2005 to December 2012, we matched 584 U.S. nonfinancial corporations with the PPI data base. On average, these firms have about 670 establishments reporting their price data to the BLS on almost 3,700 individual goods in an average month. Though sizable, our matched PPI–Compustat panel represent only a portion of the full PPI sample, which, on average, includes about 20,000 establishments, reporting data on about 90,000 goods in an average month.

To construct monthly inflation rates for these firms, we use quality-adjusted good-level prices, which control for potential changes in product quality over time. Specifically, letting $p_{i,j,t}^*$ denote the recorded transaction price of good i produced by firm j and $p_{i,j,t}^b$ the corresponding "base" price—which takes into account changes in the item's quality over time—we define the *quality-adjusted* good-level price as $p_{i,j,t} \equiv \frac{p_{i,j,t}^*}{p_{i,j,t}^b}$. The good-level inflation rate in month t—denoted by $\pi_{i,j,t}$—is then computed as

$$\pi_{i,j,t} = \Delta \log p_{i,j,t} = \Delta \log \left(\frac{p_{i,j,t}^*}{p_{i,j,t}^b} \right), \tag{1}$$

where $\Delta x_t \equiv x_t - x_{t-1}$. We also use the quality-adjusted good-level prices to calculate other price change characteristics, such as positive/negative price changes, frequency of price changes, and frequency of positive/negative price changes.[7]

Although the matched PPI–Compustat sample includes less than 600 firms, these firms tend to be appreciably larger than a typical Compustat firm (see Appendix A.2). As a result, the matched sample is representative of the U.S. economy as a whole in a number of dimensions. Panel (a) of Figure 1 shows the weighted-average of good-level inflation rates calculated using the full PPI and

---

[6]As shown by Nakamura and Steinsson (2008), however, the frequency of price changes in the narrow-item categories that are both in the CPI and PPI data sets are fairly highly correlated.

[7]To mitigate the effect of outliers on our results, we drop all observations with absolute monthly inflation rates in excess of 100 percent from both the matched PPI–Compustat and the full PPI data sets (Appendix A.1 provides a detailed comparison of the key cross-sectional price change characteristics between the two data sets).

Figure 1: Comparing Data with Broader Aggregates

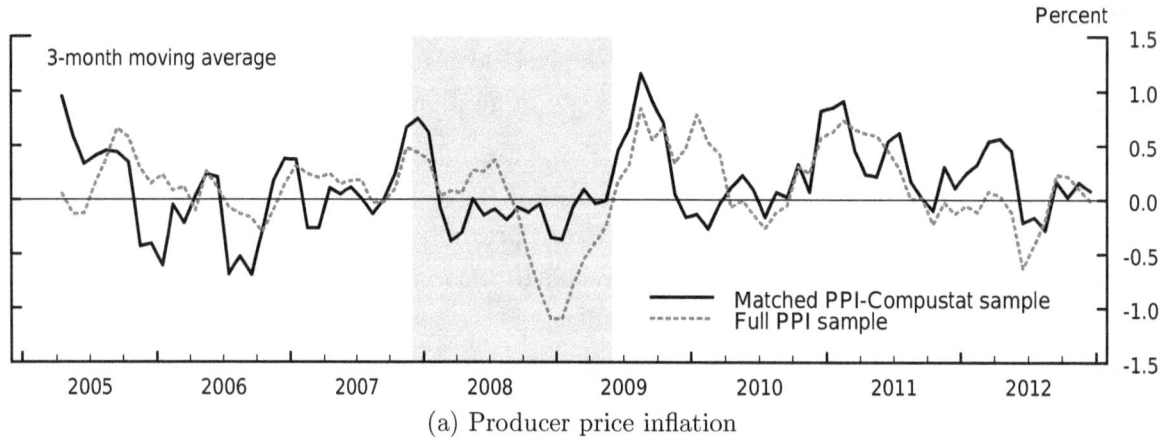

(a) Producer price inflation

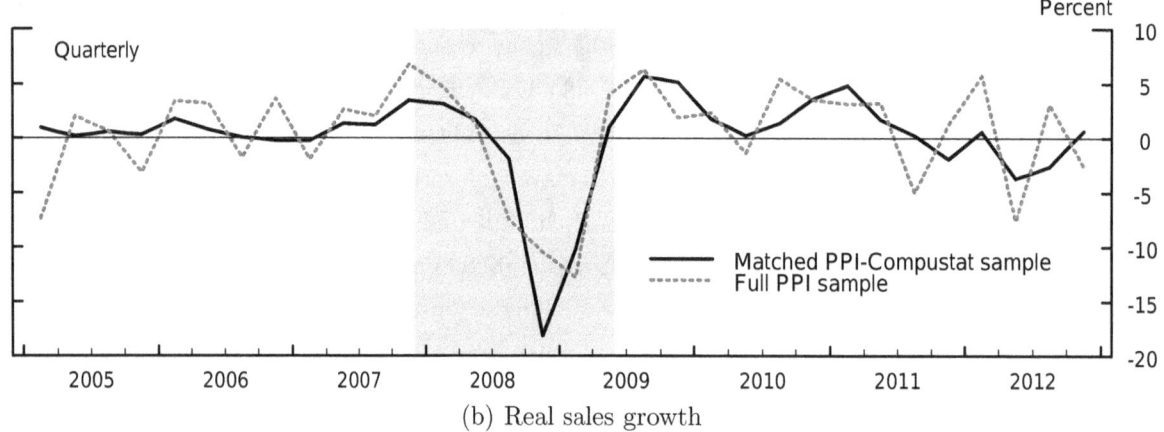

(b) Real sales growth

NOTE: The solid line in panel (a) depicts the weighted-average of monthly good-level inflation rates for the sample of 584 firms in the matched PPI–Compustat sample, while the dotted line depicts the corresponding inflation calculated using the full PPI sample. The solid line in panel (b) depicts the quarterly weighted-average growth rate of real sales for the sample of 584 firms in the matched PPI–Compustat sample, while the dotted line depicts the corresponding growth of real sales calculated using the sample of all U.S. nonfinancial firms in Compustat. The shaded vertical bar represents the 2007–09 recession as dated by the NBER.

SOURCES: Authors' calculations based on Bureau of Labor Statistics Producer Price Index (PPI) data and S&P Compustat.

the matched PPI–Compustat samples.[8] The average inflation rate based on the subset of publicly traded firms is somewhat noisier compared with the overall PPI inflation rate, but the two series are positively correlated ($\hat{\rho} = 0.51$) and in broad terms capture the same cyclical behavior of prices.[9]

---

[8]The weights used to aggregate the good-level inflation rates in each month t are the product of the relative weight of a good in the establishment's production structure and the relative weight of the establishment as measured by its total shipments.

[9]The more pronounced drop in producer prices during the latter patter of the Great Recession recorded in the full PPI data set largely reflects the fact the matched PPI–Compustat sample omits a number of goods that experienced out-sized price declines during this period. In particular, goods with massive price declines during this period are heavily concentrated in the following (3-digit NAICS) industries: Food & Beverage Stores (445); Gasoline Stations

Panel (b), in contrast, compares the weighted-average growth rate of (real) sales for the matched PPI–Compustat sample with that of all nonfinancial firms in Compustat. While the aggregate sales growth based on the limited subset of firms is again somewhat more volatile, the two series exhibit a high degree of comovement ($\hat{\rho} = 0.75$), especially during the economic downturn.

2.2 Price Dynamics by Financial and Product-Market Characteristics

One of the defining features of the Great Recession was a massive disruption in the credit intermediation process, both in the arm's-length capital markets and in the form of credit intermediated through the banking sector. With regards to the latter, Bassett et al. (2014) show that a significant portion of the decline in the capacity of businesses and households to borrow from the banking sector represented a reduction in the supply of credit lines, as banks aggressively reduced their off-balance-sheet credit exposures in response to the acute pressures on their capital and liquidity positions.

In 2008, with short-term funding markets in severe turmoil, this pullback in the supply of contingent liquidity that businesses rely upon heavily exerted a significant strain on corporate balance sheets, forcing companies to turn to internal sources of liquidity (see Campello et al., 2011). As documented by Lins et al. (2010), bank credit lines are the primary source of liquidity for companies around the world, and firms use (non-operational) cash reserves as a buffer against cashflow shocks, especially during economic downturns. Given the special role that cash holdings played during the recent crisis, we use the ratio of cash and short-term investments to total assets (the liquidity ratio)—a measure of the firm's ability to turn short-term assets into cash to cover its immediate debt obligations and fund its operations—to analyze how differences in internal liquidity affected the firms' pricing behavior during this period.

To capture product-market characteristics motivated by the customer-markets theory, we follow Gourio and Rudanko (2011) and rely on sales and general administrative (SG&A) expenditures. Specifically, we use the ratio of SG&A expenditures to sales during the same period (the SGAX ratio) to identify firms that likely operate in customer markets. The SG&A expenditures include advertising expenses and costs associated with maintaining a sales force, activities that are closely associated with developing and maintaining a loyal customer base. Alternatively, a high SGAX ratio may be indicative of high fixed costs of operation and hence of a low operating efficiency. This interpretation is also consistent with our modeling framework, in which firms face increased liquidity risk owing to high fixed and hence inflexible cost structures. In a dynamic pricing model, such firms have a natural incentive to increase prices during periods when external financing is costly and internal liquidity is scarce.

7

Table 1: Summary Statistics of Price Change Characteristics
(*By Selected Financial and Product-Market Characteristics*)

Variable (percent)	Low Liquidity Firms		High Liquidity Firms	
	Mean	SD	Mean	SD
Inflation	0.17	4.09	0.05	4.62
Positive price changes	5.45	6.97	5.46	7.82
Negative price changes	−5.52	7.89	−6.18	10.02
Freq. of price changes	19.90	39.92	19.00	39.23
Freq. of positive price changes	11.56	31.97	10.56	30.73
Freq. of negative price changes	8.34	27.64	8.44	27.80
No. of goods	5,011		3,956	
Observations	189,277		123,220	

Variable (percent)	Low SGAX Firms		High SGAX Firms	
	Mean	SD	Mean	SD
Inflation	0.18	4.52	0.04	3.96
Positive price changes	5.49	7.04	5.35	7.95
Negative price changes	−5.53	7.96	−6.49	10.76
Freq. of price changes	23.83	42.60	13.07	33.70
Freq. of positive price changes	13.61	34.29	7.46	26.28
Freq. of negative price changes	10.21	30.28	5.61	23.00
No. of goods	4,336		3,165	
Observations	188,061		124,436	

NOTE: Sample period: monthly data from 2005:M1 to 2012:M12; No. of firms = 584.
SOURCES: Authors' calculations based on BLS PPI data and Compustat.

2.2.1 Descriptive Analysis

To get a broad sense of how the strength of the firms' balance sheet interacts with their price-setting behavior, we use the liquidity ratio to classify firms in the PPI–Compustat sample into "high" and "low" liquidity categories. To minimize the switching of firms between the two categories due to seasonal or other temporary factors, we construct a trailing 12-month moving average of the liquidity ratio in month $t-1$. We then sort firms into the two categories based on whether the firm's liquidity ratio is above/below the median of its distribution in that period.[10] We use the same method to identify firms with a high (low) intensity of SG&A spending. Table 1 summarizes the first two moments of the (good-level) price change characteristics—measured from month $t-1$ to month t—for the various categories of firms over the entire 2005–12 period.

Focusing first on the financial dimension, prices of goods produced by firms with relatively ample

---

(447); and to a somewhat lesser extent Utilities (221).

[10]The PPI data are monthly, whereas the Compustat data are quarterly but are recorded in months given by the firm's fiscal year. In merging the two data sets, we are thus able to preserve the monthly frequency of the PPI data.

internal liquidity increase at a slower rate, on average, compared with prices of goods produced by their low liquidity counterparts. In an accounting sense, the average inflation differential of 12 basis points per month reflects the fact that the average price decline at high liquidity firms is about 6.2 percent per month, whereas at low liquidity firms, the average price decline is only 5.5 percent. These differences in the average inflation rates between financially strong and weak firms do not reflect differences in the extensive margin of price adjustment, as the average frequency of price changes—both overall and directional—is very similar between the two types of firms.

As shown in the bottom panel of the table, pricing dynamics also differ across firms with varying intensity of SG&A spending. Prices of goods produced by firms with a high SGAX ratio are estimated to rise at an average rate of only 4 basis points per month, compared with an 18 basis points rate of increase at firms with a low SGAX ratio. This systematic inflation differential primarily reflects larger average price cuts by the high SGAX-ratio firms (6.5 percent), compared with those at the low SGAX-ratio firms (5.5 percent). The intensity of SG&A spending is also correlated with the frequency with which firms adjust their prices. On average, high SGAX-ratio firms exhibit a markedly lower frequency of price adjustment compared with their low SGAX-ratio counterparts (7 percent vs. 14 percent); moreover this difference extends to both positive and negative price changes. The low frequency of price adjustment and hence relatively stable prices exhibited by high SGAX-ratio firms is consistent with the view that these firms engage in long-term customer relationships (see Blinder et al., 1998).

Our next descriptive exercise zeroes in on the differences in inflation dynamics between these types of firms during the Great Recession. In an effort to abstract from the effects of shocks affecting firms in different industries, we work with firm-specific *industry-adjusted* inflation rates—denoted by $\tilde{\pi}_{j,t}$—defined as

$$\tilde{\pi}_{j,t} = \sum_{i=1}^{N_{j,t}} w_{i,j,t} \times \left[\pi_{i,j,t} - \pi_t^{IND} \right],$$

where $\pi_{i,j,t}$ is the (quality-adjusted) monthly inflation rate for good i produced by firm j (see equation 1), $N_{j,t}$ is the number of goods by firm j that are included in the PPI, $0 < w_{i,j,t} \leq 1$ is the relative weight of good i within the total shipments of firm j; and π_t^{IND} is the (quality-adjusted) average inflation rate in the 2-digit NAICS industry corresponding to good i.[11]

As before, we use a trailing 12-month moving average of the liquidity (SGAX) ratio in month $t-1$ to sort firms into low/high liquidity (SGAX) categories. Especially in the financial dimension, sorting firms according to their average liquidity ratio over the course of the previous year mitigates concerns about the endogeneity between the firms' financial health and their pricing behavior during the crisis. For each group of firms, we then compute the weighted-average monthly inflation rate,

---

[11]Formally, $w_{i,j,t} = w_{i,j,t}^* \times \theta_{j,t}$, where $w_{i,j,t}^*$ denotes the relative weight of good i in the production structure of firm j (as recorded by the BLS), and $\theta_{j,t}$ is an adjustment factor that takes into account the fact that when merging the PPI data base with Compustat more than one PPI respondent may fall within the definition of the Compustat firm j. To take into account this feature of the data, the adjustment factor equals the relative value of shipments of one PPI respondent with respect to all other respondents within the same Compustat firm unit. It is also important to note that the (2-digit NAICS) industry-specific inflation rates (π_t^{IND}) are constructed using the entire PPI data base and not just the good-level price data corresponding to the matched PPI–Compustat sample.

Figure 2: Industry-Adjusted Producer Price Inflation
(*By Financial and Product-Market Characteristics*)

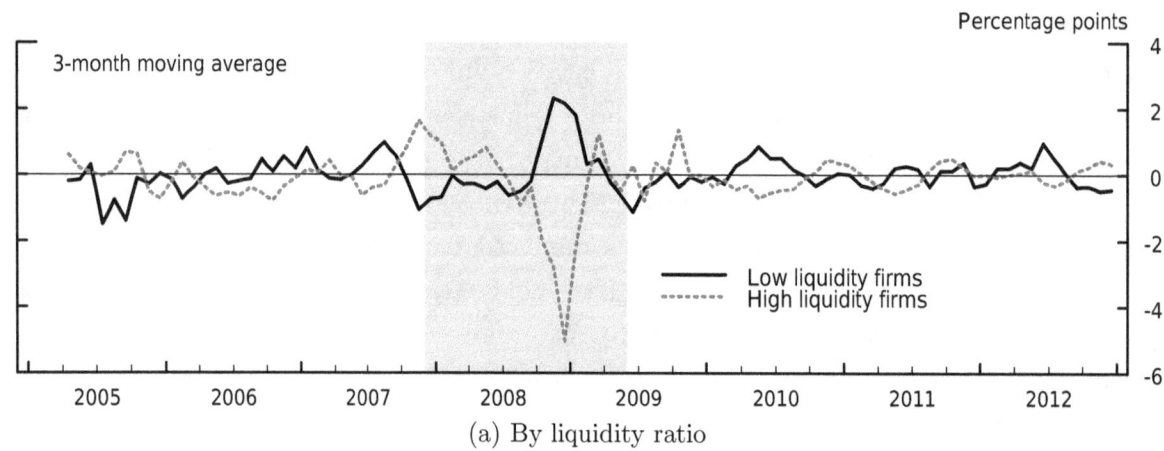

(a) By liquidity ratio

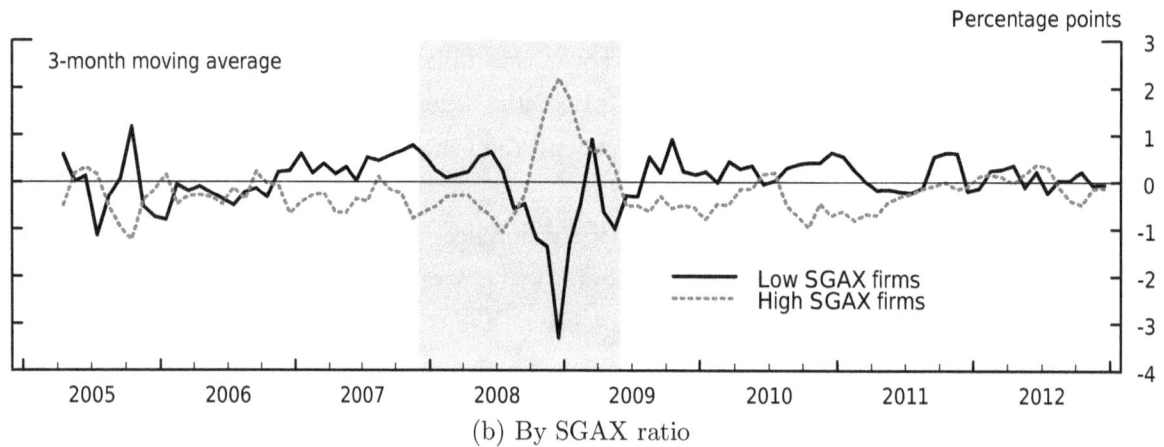

(b) By SGAX ratio

NOTE: The solid (dotted) line in panel (a) depicts the weighted-average industry-adjusted inflation rate for low (high) liquidity firms. The solid (dotted) line in panel (b) depicts the weighted-average industry-adjusted inflation rate for low (high) SGAX firms. All series are seasonally adjusted. The shaded vertical bar represents the 2007–09 recession as dated by the NBER.
SOURCES: Authors' calculations based on BLS PPI data and Compustat.

with the weights equal to the nominal value of sales in month $t-1$, as recorded by Compustat. In presenting these results, we smooth the resulting average monthly inflation rates using a 3-month moving average filter, which eliminates some of the high-frequency noise from the series.

As shown in panel (a) of Figure 2, there is a sharp divergence in the behavior of industry-adjusted inflation rates between high and low liquidity firms during the acute phase of the crisis in late 2008: Liquidity constrained firms significantly increased prices—relative to industry trends—whereas their unconstrained counterparts substantially lowered prices. The differences in the price-setting behavior between financially weak and strong firms are large in economic terms—by the end of 2008, average prices at liquidity constrained firms have jumped more than 7 percentage points

10

(not at an annual rate) relative to those at liquidity unconstrained firms. Outside this period of financial turmoil, however, the inflation patterns between these two categories of firms do not exhibit any clear systematic differences.

These results are difficult to reconcile with the standard price-adjustment mechanism emphasized by the New Keynesian literature, a paradigm where firms' financial conditions play no role in determining price-setting behavior. In the absence of large unobservable markup shocks, standard calibrations of these models imply a significant broad-based decline in producer prices in response to a contraction in output of the magnitude experienced by the U.S. economy in the latter part of 2008 (see Hall, 2011; King and Watson, 2012). Moreover, if a low (pre-determined) liquidity ratio—which is used to measure the strength of the firms' balance sheets—was indicative of weakness in demand, one would expect liquidity constrained firms to lower prices even more relative to firms with ample internal liquidity. However, we observe exactly the opposite pattern in the data.

On the other hand, the differential price dynamics between liquidity constrained and unconstrained firms during the crisis are consistent with the findings of Anderson et al. (2014), who document that a large retailer increases its regular prices more frequently when local labor market conditions deteriorate. They conjecture that this result may be due to managers raising prices to meet short-term revenue and profit targets in the face of falling sales, a strategy that can be effective if demand is relatively inelastic. Given that our sample of firms is far more representative of the production-side of the U.S. economy, the above results suggest that differences in the firms' internal liquidity positions may have a considerably more pervasive effect on their pricing behavior, especially during periods of widespread financial distress.

An almost equally striking difference in inflation dynamics emerges in panel (b) of Figure 2, which depicts the same information for firms sorted by the intensity of their SG&A spending. High SGAX firms—which purportedly operate in the customer-markets environment—also increased prices during the nadir of the crisis. In contrast, low SGAX firms lowered prices during this period. While the price response of the low SGAX firms is consistent with the standard competitive market price dynamics, the relative price increase of the high SGAX firms supports the customer-markets hypothesis, in that firms operating in such an environment will raise prices during a liquidity crunch at the expense of future market shares. As noted above, an alternative hypothesis would argue that a substantial part of the firm's SG&A expenditures reflects overhead costs and that a high SGAX ratio is indicative of a low operational efficiency. Such firms, facing both a liquidity squeeze and falling cashflows, may be forced to boost prices in order to cover immediate debt obligations and help fund operations.

Although fairly short lived, these differences in relative *inflation* during the crisis have significant consequences for the subsequent behavior of relative *prices*. Moreover, they are not an artifact of firms moving from one category to another or firms altering their liquidity positions as the crisis unfolds. To abstract from these effects, we sorted firms into low/high liquidity categories (or low/high SGAX categories) based on their average liquidity ratio (or SGAX ratio) in 2006—that is, well before the onset of the financial crisis. As shown in panel (a) of Figure 3, the weighted

Figure 3: Industry-Adjusted Producer Prices
(*By Financial and Product-Market Characteristics as of 2006*)

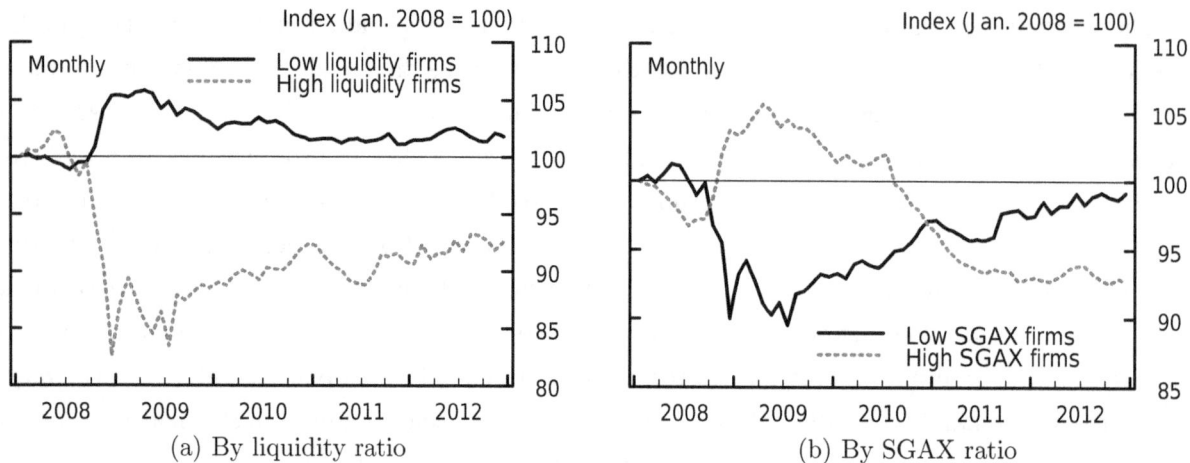

(a) By liquidity ratio (b) By SGAX ratio

NOTE: The solid (dotted) line in panel (a) depicts the cumulative weighted-average industry-adjusted inflation rates for low (high) liquidity firms as of 2006. The solid (dotted) line in panel (b) depicts cumulative weighted-average industry-adjusted inflation rates for low (high) SGAX firms as of 2006.
SOURCES: Authors' calculations based on BLS PPI data and Compustat.

average of prices charged by the ex ante liquidity constrained firms remains persistently above that charged by the firms that had more liquid balance sheets in 2006, even when taking into account the industry-level price dynamics. The divergence in the industry-adjusted prices between the low and high SGAX firms shown in panel (b), by contrast, is somewhat less persistent, reflecting, in part, the significantly higher average rate of good-level inflation at firms with a low intensity of SG&A spending (see Table 1).

As emphasized by Bils et al. (2013), disinflationary pressures during the Great Recession were most pronounced in nondurable goods manufacturing. As shown in Appendix A.3, our micro-level data also indicate that the deflationary pressures during the recent financial crisis were concentrated primarily in nondurable goods manufacturing. Moreover, relative price deflation within that sector appears to reflect solely a large price cut by liquidity unconstrained firms or firms with a low level of SG&A expenditures relative to sales. In contrast, nondurable goods manufacturers with weak balance sheets or those with a high SGAX ratio significantly increased—relative to industry trends—prices during the crisis.

The fact that the difference in relative inflation dynamics between low and high liquidity firms is apparent only in nondurable goods manufacturing provides additional support for our hypothesis that the strategic interaction of firms operating in customer markets and facing some form of financial distortions has a significant effect on the behavior of inflation in periods of financial turmoil. First, this sector is more likely to include industries characterized by business-to-business markets for intermediate goods, where customer retention and customer acquisition play key roles in firms' pricing decisions. This result also comports with the notion that nondurables typically

12

involve items that are purchased relatively frequently and whose purchases are thus more likely to be influenced by habits and past experience, factors at the center of the customer-markets theory. In contrast, one would expect customers to be more price "sensitive" and less influenced by past habits when buying big-ticket durable goods that are purchased infrequently.

2.2.2 Multivariate Analysis

With these stylized facts in hand, we now turn to regression analysis to examine how differences in the strength of firms' balance sheet and the intensity of SG&A spending affect their price-setting behavior. This approach allows us to use micro-level data to estimate the effect of these two factors on the firms' actual price-setting behavior, while explicitly controlling for other firm-specific and aggregate factors that may influence firms' pricing decisions over the course of a business cycle.

In this analysis, we consider two pricing decision variables: (1) the firm's observed decision to change prices at the good level—a variable representing the extensive margin of price adjustment; and (2) good-level price inflation, which reflects the combined effect of the extensive and intensive margins. In the first case, we estimate a multinomial logit regression

$$\Pr\left(\mathrm{sgn}[p_{i,j,t+3} - p_{i,j,t}]\right) = \begin{cases} - \\ 0 \\ + \end{cases} = \Lambda(\mathbf{X}_{j,t}, \mathbf{Z}_t; \boldsymbol{\theta}), \tag{2}$$

where $\mathrm{sgn}[p_{i,j,t+3} - p_{i,j,t}]$ is a discrete variable that equals "$-$" if the price of good i (produced by firm j) decreased between months t and $t+3$; "$+$" if the price of good i increased between months t and $t+3$; and "0" if the price of good i did not change during this 3-month period. In the second case, we estimate a linear pricing regression

$$\pi_{i,j,t+3}^{3m} = \boldsymbol{\beta}_1' \mathbf{X}_{j,t} + \boldsymbol{\beta}_2' \mathbf{Z}_t + \eta_j + u_{i,j,t+3}, \tag{3}$$

where $\pi_{i,j,t+3}^{3m} = \log p_{i,j,t+3} - \log p_{i,j,t}$ is the (quality-adjusted) inflation rate of good i from month t to month $t+3$. The use of 3-month changes (from t to $t+3$) reflects the fact that the firm-level Compustat variables are available only at the quarterly frequency.

The good-level dependent variables in equations (2) and (3) are modeled as functions of firm-specific ($\mathbf{X}_{j,t}$) and aggregate ($\mathbf{Z}_t$) covariates. The key firm-specific explanatory variables are the liquidity and SGAX ratios, denoted by $\mathrm{LIQ}_{j,t}$ and $\mathrm{SGAX}_{j,t}$, respectively. To capture the differential effect of these two variables on the firms' pricing decisions during the financial crisis, we include the interaction terms $\mathrm{LIQ}_{j,t} \times \mathrm{CRISIS}_t$ and $\mathrm{SGAX}_{j,t} \times \mathrm{CRISIS}_t$ in both specifications, where CRISIS_t denotes an indicator variable that equals 1 in 2008 and 0 otherwise.

Additional firm-specific explanatory variables are the 12-month growth of nominal sales ($\log(S_{j,t}/S_{j,t-12})$) and the current inventory-sales ratio ($[I/S]_{j,t}$); the former controls for the recent changes in demand, while the latter captures liquidity demand that may arise from the need to finance inventories (see Barth and Ramey, 2001). Both specifications also include the 3-month,

Table 2: Firm-Level Characteristics and Price-Setting Behavior
(*Financial Crisis vs. Normal Times*)

| Explanatory Variables | (1) | | (2) |
	$+$	$-$	π^{3m}
$\mathrm{LIQ}_{j,t} \times [\mathrm{CRISIS}_t = 1]$	-0.350^{***}	0.137	-0.030^{***}
	(0.123)	(0.092)	(0.011)
$\mathrm{LIQ}_{j,t} \times [\mathrm{CRISIS}_t = 0]$	-0.018	0.067	-0.002
	(0.074)	(0.055)	(0.007)
$\mathrm{SGAX}_{j,t} \times [\mathrm{CRISIS}_t = 1]$	-0.267^{***}	-0.263^{***}	0.006
	(0.080)	(0.100)	(0.008)
$\mathrm{SGAX}_{j,t} \times [\mathrm{CRISIS}_t = 0]$	-0.339^{***}	-0.281^{***}	0.003
	(0.078)	(0.071)	(0.003)
$\log(S_{j,t}/S_{j,t-12})$	-0.007	-0.032^{*}	0.001
	(0.018)	(0.018)	(0.003)
$[I/S]_{j,t}$	-0.019	-0.015	0.002
	(0.020)	(0.023)	(0.003)
$\pi_t^{IND(3m)}$	1.024^{***}	-0.173	0.059
	(0.321)	(0.180)	(0.042)
Time fixed effects[a]	$<.001$	$<.001$	$<.001$
Firm fixed effects[b]	$.$	$.$	$<.001$

NOTE: Sample period: 2005:M1 to 2012:12 at a quarterly frequency; No. of firms = 556; Obs. = 98,813. Both specifications also include the interaction terms (not reported) $\mathrm{LIQ}_{j,t} \times \log(P_t^{OIL}/P_{t-3}^{OIL})$ and $\mathrm{SGAX}_{j,t} \times \log(P_t^{OIL}/P_{t-3}^{OIL})$, where P_t^{OIL} denotes the price of oil. Robust asymptotic standard errors reported in parentheses are clustered at the firm level: * $p < .10$; ** $p < .05$; and *** $p < .01$.
[a] p-value for the test of null hypothesis that time fixed effects are jointly equal to zero.
[b] p-value for the test of null hypothesis that firm fixed effects are jointly equal to zero.

3-digit NAICS inflation corresponding to good i ($\pi_t^{IND(3m)}$) to control for the industry-level pricing dynamics. Time fixed effects, on the other hand, capture common macroeconomic shocks. The linear pricing regression (3) also includes a firm fixed effect (η_j), which controls for differences in the unobservable firm-level characteristics (for example, differences in the average productivity growth) that can influence the firm's decision to change its prices.

In addition to the widespread seizing-up of credit markets, 2008 was also marked by a collapse in oil prices. In the second half of the year, the spot price of the West Texas Intermediate (WTI) crude—a widely used benchmark in oil pricing—fell about 70 percent. Such a large drop in oil prices was reflected in a substantial decline in the cost of energy inputs, implying a significant reduction in the firms' marginal costs, especially in the energy-intensive industries. If energy intensity of the firm's production process is positively correlated with the firm's liquidity position, then one could observe liquidity unconstrained firms lowering prices during 2008 to a greater extent than their liquidity constrained counterparts.

By the same argument, we should have observed liquidity unconstrained firms raising their prices during 2007 and the first half of 2008, a period in which the price of WTI crude more than doubled. While the evidence in panel (a) of Figure 2 does indicate that during this period high liquidity firms raised prices relative to those of their low liquidity counterparts, the difference in the industry-adjusted inflation rates for the two categories of firms is much smaller compared with that during the latter half of 2008. Nevertheless, to take into account the possibility that the firm's internal liquidity position or the intensity of their SG&A spending may be correlated with the energy intensity of the firm's production process, each specification also includes the interaction terms $\text{LIQ}_{j,t} \times \log(P_t^{OIL}/P_{t-3}^{OIL})$ and $\text{SGAX}_{j,t} \times \log(P_t^{OIL}/P_{t-3}^{OIL})$, where P_t^{OIL} denotes the spot price of WTI crude in month t. It is worth noting, though, that our results are robust to excluding these interaction terms from both specifications.

Table 2 summarizes the results from our regression analysis: The two columns of specification (1) report the (outcome-specific) marginal effects of the specified explanatory variable on the probability of upward $(+)$ and downward $(-)$ price adjustment; specification (2), in contrast, reports the corresponding effects for the overall inflation (π^{3m}).[12] According to column 1, differences in internal corporate liquidity imply significant differences in the propensity of firms to increase their prices during the recent crisis. Specifically, the point estimate of -0.350 associated with the interaction term $\text{LIQ}_{j,t} \times [\text{CRISIS}_t = 1]$ implies that in 2008, a decline in the liquidity ratio of two standard deviations around the mean (32 percentage points according to Table A-2) boosted the likelihood of a price *increase* over the subsequent 3 months—relative to the baseline case of no price change—about 11 percentage points.

In addition to being statistically highly significant, this effect is economically meaningful, as the unconditional probability of an upward price adjustment over a 3-month period is roughly 30 percent for both low and high liquidity firms (see Table 1). Thus in 2008, firms in a weak internal liquidity position were much more likely to raise their prices, compared with their financially stronger counterparts. Outside this period of financial turmoil, changes in the firms' internal liquidity positions have no discernible effect on the extensive margin of price adjustment.

In general, a high SGAX ratio implies a significantly lower probability of a subsequent price change—both upward and downward. The finding that high SGAX firms have more stable prices is consistent with the differences in the average unconditional frequencies of prices changes between low and high SGAX firms reported in Table 1. The marginal effect of the SGAX ratio on the probability of upward price adjustment during the crisis is, in absolute terms, smaller than during normal times, a result that supports the idea that firms operating in customer markets increase prices during periods of widespread financial distress. However, the difference in the estimated marginal effects of the SGAX ratio on the probability of a price increase between normal and crisis times $(-0.339$ vs. $-0.267)$ is relatively small in economic terms.

The results reported in column 2 of the table also comport with the notion that differences in firms' internal liquidity positions significantly influenced inflation outcomes during the crisis period. According to our estimates, a two standard deviation difference in the liquidity ratio across firms during this period implies a difference in the PPI price inflation of almost a full percentage point

---

[12]In the estimation of the multinomial logit regression (2), we treat $\text{sgn}[p_{i,j,t+3} - p_{i,j,t}] = 0$ as the base outcome.

Figure 4: The Effect of Liquidity and SGAX Ratios on the Probability of Price Adjustment

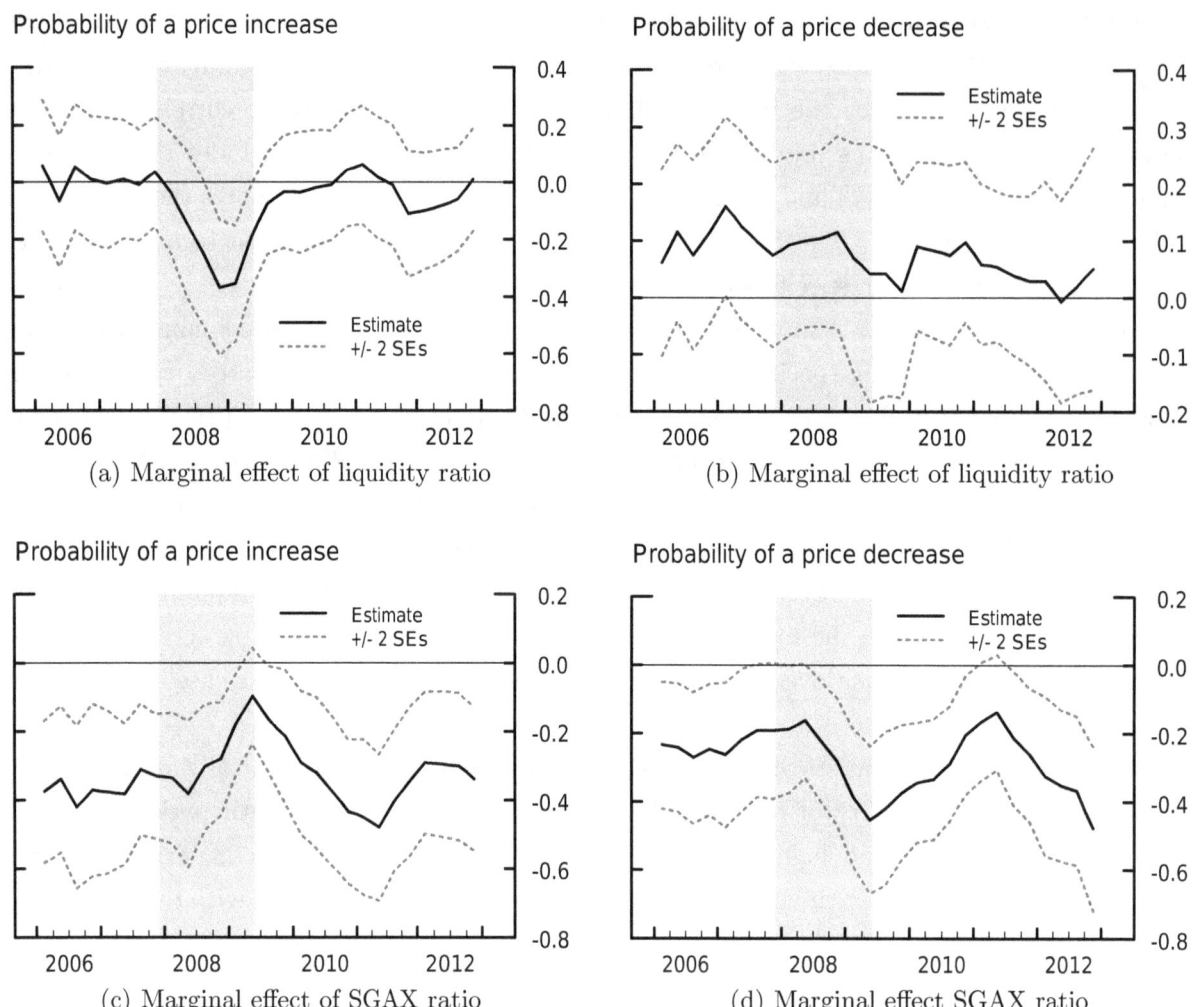

(a) Marginal effect of liquidity ratio

(b) Marginal effect of liquidity ratio

(c) Marginal effect of SGAX ratio

(d) Marginal effect SGAX ratio

NOTE: The solid lines in panels (a) and (b) depict the time-varying estimates of the (average) marginal effect of the liquidity ratio on the probability of positive and negative price changes (relative to no change), respectively. The solid lines in panels (c) and (d) depict the same information with respect to the SGAX ratio. The estimates are plotted at the end-point of the rolling four-quarter estimation window. Robust asymptotic standard errors are clustered at the firm level. The shaded vertical bar represents the 2007–09 recession as dated by the NBER.

(not at an annual rate) over the subsequent 3 months. Interestingly, differences in the SGAX ratio, although having a large effect on the probability of a price change, have no effect on the overall price inflation.

A potential concern with the above analysis is that we only allow the coefficients on the liquidity and SGAX ratios to change during the financial crisis. It is plausible that the impact of other explanatory variables is also different in such extreme economic circumstances. To examine the sensitivity of our results to this assumption, we re-estimate specifications (2) and (3) using a rolling

Figure 5: The Effect Liquidity Ratio on Producer Price Inflation

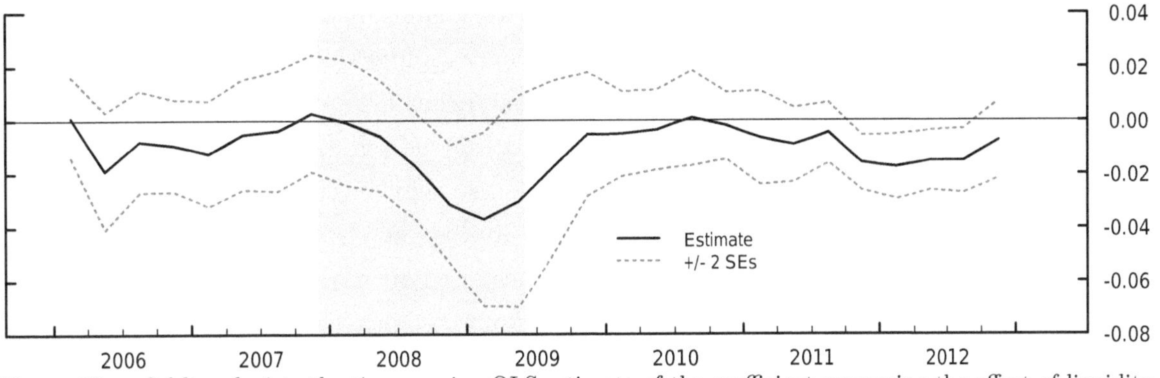

NOTE: The solid line depicts the time-varying OLS estimate of the coefficient measuring the effect of liquidity ratio on producer price inflation. The estimates are plotted at the end-point of the rolling four-quarter estimation window. Robust asymptotic standard errors are clustered at the firm level. The shaded vertical bar represents the 2007–09 recession as dated by the NBER.

four-quarter window, thereby allowing for time-series variation in all the response coefficients.[13]

Panels (a) and (b) of Figure 4 show the estimated time-varying marginal effects with respect to the liquidity ratio, while panels (c) and (d) depict those with respect to the SGAX ratio. These results further corroborate the hypothesis that differences in corporate liquidity significantly affected the propensity of firms to increase their prices during the Great Recession. As shown in panel (a), firms with low levels of internal liquidity during the crisis were much more likely to increase prices, compared with their liquidity unconstrained counterparts. Moreover, the point estimate of the marginal effect of the liquidity ratio on the probability of upward price adjustment during the nadir of the crisis in late 2008 is virtually the same as that reported in Table 2. Also consistent with our previous results, panel (b) shows that changes in the liquidity ratio have no discernible effect on the propensity of firms to lower prices—in either normal or crisis periods.

Compared with the results in Table 2, panels (c) and (d) indicate a somewhat more pronounced time variation in the effect of the SGAX ratio on the likelihood of price adjustment during the crisis. In general, a high SGAX ratio implies a significantly lower frequency of price adjustment—both upwards and downwards. However, during the financial crisis, a higher SGAX ratio implies a substantially higher probability of a price increase (panel (c)) and a substantially lower probability of a price decrease (panel (d)). These results are again consistent with an environment where customer market considerations induce firms to raise prices during periods of financial turmoil; they are also consistent with the alternative but complementary interpretation that firms with a high SGAX ratio have relatively inflexible cost structures and increase prices as a way to avoid a liquidity shortfall in the face of falling output.

Figure 5 shows the time-varying effect of the liquidity ratio on the overall price inflation. Con-

---

[13]In this case, we omit the oil interaction terms from both specifications, as these terms had no effect on the results reported in Table 2. Reflecting significantly smaller sample sizes, including the oil interaction terms in the rolling estimation reduced the precision of the estimates somewhat; point estimates were very similar, however.

sistent with our previous results, a low liquidity ratio during the crisis period foreshadows an economically and statistically significant increase in inflation over the subsequent three months. In fact, the estimate of this effect at the end of 2008 is very close to that based on the full-sample specification reported in Table 2. In other times, by contrast, differences in firms' internal liquidity positions have no discernible effect on their price-setting behavior.[14]

In sum, our empirical analysis strongly supports the notion that firms' internal liquidity positions—measured by the sum of their holdings of cash and marketable securities—played an important role in shaping their price-setting behavior during the Great Recession. The drying up of external liquidity such as commercial paper and lines of credit in response to shocks that roiled credit markets in 2008 induced firms with relatively illiquid balance sheets to significantly increase their prices, whereas their liquidity unconstrained counterparts slashed prices during the economic downturn. From a macroeconomic perspective, our results point to the interaction of financial market frictions and customer markets as a potentially important mechanism that can significantly attenuate deflationary pressures resulting from a sharp contraction in economic activity in periods of widespread credit market disruptions.

3   Model

In this section, we develop a general equilibrium model that is qualitatively able to match salient facts about the dynamics of producer prices during the nadir of the 2007–09 financial crisis. To motivate the competition for market shares implied by the customer-markets hypothesis, we consider household preferences that allow for the formation of a customer base, whereby low prices today are a form of investment into future market shares (see Rotemberg and Woodford, 1991). Specifically, we adopt the good-specific habit model of Ravn et al. (2006), which we augment with nominal rigidities in the form of quadratic adjustment costs faced by firms when changing nominal prices. Because our empirical analysis indicates that financial factors primarily affect the price-setting behavior of firms in the nondurable goods sector, we consider only perishable goods in our model formulation. To explore the influence of financial frictions on the firms' price-setting behavior, our framework also includes a tractable model of costly external finance.

Our full model, which is detailed in Appendix B.1, features heterogeneous firms. To highlight the essential mechanism at work, however, we first consider a version of the model with homogeneous firms. We then analyze the full model to study the extent to which financially weak firms—in response to an adverse financial shock—may increase prices relative to those of their financially strong counterparts, a behavior documented for the peak of the crisis in latter part of 2008. Allowing for firm heterogeneity significantly amplifies the adverse feedback loop between financial conditions and the real economy because firms with relatively strong balance sheet—and thus relatively easy access to external finance—exploit the weak financial position of their competitors by lowering prices and stealing their market share.

---

[14] As a robustness exercise, we also considered specifications where the firm-specific liquidity ratio was fixed at its 2006 level. These results were quantitatively very similar to those reported in the paper.

3.1 Preferences and Technology

The model economy contains a continuum of households indexed by $j \in [0, 1]$. Each household consumes a variety of consumption goods indexed by $i \in [0, 1]$. The preferences of households are defined over a habit-adjusted consumption bundle x_t^j and labor h_t^j as

$$\mathbb{E}_t \sum_{s=0}^{\infty} \beta^s U(x_{t+s}^j - \psi_{t+s}, h_{t+s}^j), \tag{4}$$

where the AR(1) demand shock ψ_t affects the final demand by altering the current marginal utility of consumption.

The consumption/habit aggregator is defined as

$$x_t^j \equiv \left[\int_0^1 \left(\frac{c_{it}^j}{s_{i,t-1}^\theta} \right)^{1 - \frac{1}{\eta}} di \right]^{\frac{1}{1 - \frac{1}{\eta}}}; \quad \theta < 0 \text{ and } \eta > 0, \tag{5}$$

where c_{it}^j denotes the amount of a good of variety i consumed by household j, and s_{it} is the habit stock associated with good i. The good-specific habit stock is assumed to be external and thus taken as given by consumers—that is, "keeping up with the Joneses" at the good level.[15] Specifically, we assume that the external habit evolves according to

$$s_{it} = \rho s_{i,t-1} + (1 - \rho) c_{it}; \quad 0 < \rho < 1. \tag{6}$$

The dual problem of cost minimization gives rise to a good-specific demand:

$$c_{it}^j = \left(\frac{p_{it}}{\tilde{p}_t} \right)^{-\eta} s_{i,t-1}^{\theta(1-\eta)} x_t^j, \tag{7}$$

where $p_{it} = P_{it}/P_t$ is the relative price of variety i in terms of $P_t = \left[\int_0^1 P_{it}^{1-\eta} di \right]^{1/(1-\eta)}$, and the externality-adjusted composite price index $\tilde{p}_t$ is given by

$$\tilde{p}_t = \left[\int_0^1 \left(p_{it} s_{i,t-1}^\theta \right)^{1-\eta} di \right]^{\frac{1}{1-\eta}}. \tag{8}$$

The supply side of the economy is characterized by a continuum of monopolistically competitive firms producing a differentiated variety of goods indexed by $i \in [0, 1]$. The production technology is given by

$$y_{it} = \left(\frac{A_t}{a_{it}} h_{it} \right)^\alpha - \phi; \quad 0 < \alpha \le 1, \tag{9}$$

where A_t is aggregate productivity, and a_{it} is an idiosyncratic (i.i.d.) productivity shock, dis-

---

[15]In addition to being mathematically more tractable, the assumption of external habits avoids the time-inconsistency problem of firm price setting associated with good-specific internal habits (see Nakamura and Steinsson, 2011).

tributed as $\log a_{it} \sim N(-0.5\sigma^2, \sigma^2)$, with the associated CDF denoted by $F(a)$. Note that we allow the production technology to exhibit either decreasing or constant returns to scale. In addition, we assume that production is subject to fixed operating costs—denoted by ϕ—which makes it possible for firms to incur negative operating income, thereby creating a liquidity squeeze if external financing is costly. Although we do not explicitly model the balance sheet of the firm, implicitly, these fixed costs can include "long-term debt payments," a coupon payment to perpetual bond holders. Thus broadly speaking, the presence of fixed operating costs captures the possibility of a debt overhang.

Firms make pricing and production decisions to maximize the present value of discounted dividends. Our timing assumptions imply that firms must commit to pricing decisions—and hence production—based on all aggregate information available within the period, but prior to the realization of their idiosyncratic productivity shock. Based on this aggregate information, firms post prices, take orders from customers, and plan production based on *expected* marginal costs. Firms then realize actual marginal cost and hire labor to meet the demand. Labor must be paid within the period and in the presence of fixed operating costs, the firm's ex post profits may be too low to cover the total cost of production. In that case, the firm must raise external funds.

To introduce a wedge between the cost of internal and external finance in a tractable manner, we focus on equity as the sole source of external finance. That is, firms can obtain external funds only by issuing new equity, a process that involves dilution costs reflecting agency problems in financial markets. Formally, we assume that equity finance involves a constant per-unit dilution cost $\varphi_t \in (0, 1)$ per dollar of equity issued. Dilution costs are indexed by time to allow for exogenous changes in financing costs—that is, financial shocks. To keep the model tractable, we abstract from firm savings decisions by assuming that all dividends are paid out within the period.[16] This formulation of costly external finance allows us to highlight the basic mechanism within a framework that deviates only slightly from the standard good-specific habit model. In particular, in our model, all firms are identical ex ante, and as a result, only firms with an idiosyncratic productivity shock below an endogenous threshold incur negative profits and are forced to issue new equity.

3.2 Profit Maximization

We now turn to the firm's problem, which, for simplicity, we describe abstracting from nominal rigidities. We then consider the implications of adding frictions to nominal price setting, which allows us to highlight the model's implications for the Phillips curve. The firm's objective is to maximize the expected present value of a dividend flow, $\mathbb{E}_0 \left[\sum_{t=0}^{\infty} m_{0,t} \, d_{it} \right]$, where d_{it} denotes the (real) dividend payout when positive and equity issuance when negative, and $m_{0,t}$ is the stochastic discount factor. Note that the presence of equity dilution costs φ_t implies that when a firm issues a

---

[16]Allowing for costly equity financing and precautionary cash holding is of obvious interest but would make the *distribution* of firms' liquid asset holdings a state variable. We leave this nontrivial extension for future research. However, our full model with firm heterogeneity can be thought of as representing an economy in which a certain proportion of firms have accumulated sufficient liquidity, so as to behave in an unconstrained manner. As shown in Section 5, this does not eliminate the main mechanism of our model.

notional amount of equity $d_{it} < 0$, actual cash intake from the issuance is reduced to $-(1 - \varphi_t)d_{it}$.

The firm's problem is subject to the flow-of-funds constraint:

$$0 = p_{it}c_{it} - w_t h_{it} - d_{it} + \varphi_t \min\{0, d_{it}\}; \tag{10}$$

and given the monopolistically competitive product markets, the demand constraint specified in equation (7). Formally, letting λ_{it}, ν_{it}, κ_{it}, and ξ_{it} denote the Lagrange multipliers associated with equations (6), (7), (9), and (10), respectively, the Lagrangian associated with the firm's problem is given by

$$
\begin{aligned}
\mathcal{L} = \mathbb{E}_0 \sum_{t=0}^{\infty} m_{0,t} &\left\{ d_{it} + \kappa_{it} \left[\left(\frac{A_t}{a_{it}} h_{it} \right)^{\alpha} - \phi - c_{it} \right] \right. \\
&+ \xi_{it} \left[p_{it}c_{it} - w_t h_{it} - d_{it} + \varphi_t \min\{0, d_{it}\} \right] \\
&\left. + \nu_{it} \left[\left(\frac{p_{it}}{\tilde{p}_t} \right)^{-\eta} s_{i,t-1}^{\theta(1-\eta)} x_t - c_{it} \right] + \lambda_{it} \left[\rho s_{i,t-1} + (1-\rho)c_{it} - s_{it} \right] \right\}.
\end{aligned}
\tag{11}
$$

The firm's optimal choices of its decision variables are summarized by the following first-order conditions:

$$d_{it}: \quad \xi_{it} = \begin{cases} 1 & \text{if } d_{it} \geq 0 \\ 1/(1-\varphi_t) & \text{if } d_{it} < 0 \end{cases} \tag{12}$$

$$h_{it}: \quad \kappa_{it} = \xi_{it}a_{it}\left(\frac{w_t}{\alpha A_t}\right)(c_{it} + \phi)^{\frac{1-\alpha}{\alpha}} \tag{13}$$

$$c_{it}: \quad \mathbb{E}_t^a[\nu_{it}] = \mathbb{E}_t^a[\xi_{it}]p_{it} - \mathbb{E}_t^a[\kappa_{it}] + (1-\rho)\mathbb{E}_t^a[\lambda_{it}] \tag{14}$$

$$s_{it}: \quad \mathbb{E}_t^a[\lambda_{it}] = \rho\mathbb{E}_t^a[m_{t,t+1}\lambda_{i,t+1}] + \theta(1-\eta)\mathbb{E}_t\left[m_{t,t+1}\mathbb{E}_{t+1}^a[\nu_{i,t+1}]\left(\frac{c_{i,t+1}}{s_{it}}\right)\right] \tag{15}$$

$$p_{it}: \quad 0 = \mathbb{E}_t^a[\xi_{it}] - \eta\frac{\mathbb{E}_t^a[\nu_{it}]}{p_{it}}. \tag{16}$$

Implicit in the last three conditions is the assumption that the firm makes pricing and production decisions prior to the realization of the idiosyncratic productivity shock a_{it}. Accordingly, these first-order conditions involve the expected shadow values of internal funds ($\mathbb{E}_t^a[\xi_{it}]$), marginal sales ($\mathbb{E}_t^a[\nu_{it}]$), and habit stock ($\mathbb{E}_t^a[\lambda_{it}]$), where the expectations are formed using all aggregate information up to time t. In contrast, the realized values ξ_{it} and a_{it} enter the efficiency conditions (12) and (13) without the expectations operator because dividend payouts (or new equity issuance) and labor hiring decisions are made after the realization of the idiosyncratic productivity shock.[17]

Under risk-neutrality and with i.i.d. idiosyncratic productivity shocks, the timing convention adopted above implies that firms are identical ex ante.[18] Hence, we focus on a symmetric equilib-

---

[17]The labor demand $h_{it} = \left(\frac{a_{it}}{A_t}\right)(c_{it} + \phi)^{\frac{1}{\alpha}}$ is substituted into equation (13) after deriving the first-order condition.

[18]A similar timing convention has been used by Kiley and Sim (2012) in the context of financial intermediation.

21

rium, in which all monopolistically competitive firms choose the identical relative price ($p_{it} = 1$), production scale ($c_{it} = c_t$), and habit stock ($s_{it} = s_t$). However, the distributions of labor inputs (h_{it}) and dividend payouts (d_{it}) are non-degenerate and depend on the realization of the idiosyncratic productivity shock.

3.3 Value of Internal Funds and the Customer Base

Define the equity issuance trigger a_t^E as the level of idiosyncratic productivity that satisfies the flow-of-funds constraint (10) when dividends are exactly zero:

$$a_t^E = \frac{c_t}{(c_t + \phi)^{\frac{1}{\alpha}}} \frac{A_t}{w_t}. \tag{17}$$

The first-order condition for dividends (equation 12) implies that because of costly external financing, the realized shadow value of internal funds increases from 1 to $1/(1 - \varphi_t) > 1$, when the realization of the idiosyncratic productivity shock is greater than the threshold value a_t^E:

$$\xi(a_{it}) = \begin{cases} 1 & \text{if } a_{it} \leq a_t^E \\ 1/(1 - \varphi_t) & \text{if } a_{it} > a_t^E. \end{cases} \tag{18}$$

Let z_t^E denote the standardized value of a_t^E; that is, $z_t^E = \sigma^{-1}\left(\log a_t^E + 0.5\sigma^2\right)$. The expected shadow value of internal funds can then be expressed as

$$\mathbb{E}_t^a[\xi_{it}] = \int_0^{a_t^E} dF(a) + \int_{a_t^E}^{\infty} \frac{1}{1 - \varphi_t} dF(a) = 1 + \left[\frac{\varphi_t}{1 - \varphi_t}\right][1 - \Phi(z_t^E)] \geq 1, \tag{19}$$

where $\Phi(\cdot)$ denotes the standard normal CDF.

The expected shadow value of internal funds is strictly greater than one as long as equity issuance is costly ($\varphi_t > 0$) and the firm faces idiosyncratic liquidity risk ($\sigma > 0$). This makes the firm de facto risk averse when making its pricing decision. Setting the price too low and taking an imprudently large number of orders exposes the firm to the risk of incurring negative operating income, which must be financed through costly equity issuance.[19]

Consider first the case with no habits, so that $\theta = 0$, in which case $\lambda_{it} = 0$. By combining the first-order conditions (13), (14), and (16), we can express the pricing rule as

$$p_{it} = \frac{\eta}{\eta - 1} \frac{\mathbb{E}_t^a[\xi_{it} a_{it}]}{\mathbb{E}_t^a[\xi_{it}]} \left[\frac{w_t}{\alpha A_t}(c_{it} + \phi)^{\frac{1-\alpha}{\alpha}}\right], \tag{20}$$

where, in the symmetric equilibrium, $p_{it} = 1$ and $c_{it} = c_t$. With frictionless financial markets,

---

[19]Equation (17) imposes the symmetric equilibrium. From the firm's perspective, raising prices increases profits and hence reduces the cost of external finance if $\frac{p_{it} c_{it}}{w_t h_{it}}$ is increasing in the price charged. Given the production function (9), this is true if $1 - \eta\left(1 - \frac{1}{\alpha}\frac{c_t}{c_t + \varphi_t}\right) > 0$, where η is the short-run demand elasticity. Because the term in parentheses is close to zero, this condition is satisfied in any reasonable calibration of the model.

22

$\mathbb{E}_t^a[\xi_{it}] = \mathbb{E}_t^a[\xi_{it}a_{it}] = 1$, and we obtain the standard result that firms set prices as a constant markup over marginal cost, the term in brackets. It is straightforward to show that

$$\frac{\mathbb{E}_t^a[\xi_{it}a_{it}]}{\mathbb{E}_t^a[\xi_{it}]} = 1 + \frac{\mathbb{COV}_t^a[\xi_{it}a_{it}]}{\mathbb{E}_t^a[\xi_{it}]} = \frac{1 - \varphi_t\Phi(z_t^E - \sigma)}{1 - \varphi_t\Phi(z_t^E)} > 1, \tag{21}$$

where the second equality follows from properties of the log-normal distribution.

The result that $\mathbb{COV}_t^a[\xi_{it}a_{it}] > 0$ is due to the additional risk associated with low internal liquidity. The firm hedges against this risk by setting a higher markup relative to marginal cost. Because the right-hand side of equation (18) is increasing in dilution cost φ_t, this mechanism introduces a form of the cost channel into the model, through which financial distortions raise marginal costs—*inclusive of expected financing costs*—and thereby reduce profit margins. Define the financially adjusted markup as the inverse of marginal cost, inclusive of expected financing costs:

$$\tilde{\mu}_t = \frac{1}{\frac{\mathbb{E}_t^a[\xi_{it}a_{it}]}{\mathbb{E}_t^a[\xi_{it}]}\left[\frac{w_t}{\alpha A_t}(c_{it} + \phi)^{\frac{1-\alpha}{\alpha}}\right]}. \tag{22}$$

The pricing rule in equation (20) then implies that, in the absence of customer markets, firms set prices as a constant markup over the *financially adjusted* marginal cost $1/\tilde{\mu}_t$.

With customer markets, $\lambda_{it} > 0$, the first-order conditions (13) and (14) imply that the value of marginal sales ν_{it} satisfies:

$$\frac{\mathbb{E}_t^a[\nu_{it}]}{\mathbb{E}_t^a[\xi_{it}]} = \frac{\tilde{\mu}_t - 1}{\tilde{\mu}_t} + (1 - \rho)\frac{\mathbb{E}_t^a[\lambda_{it}]}{\mathbb{E}_t^a[\xi_{it}]}, \tag{23}$$

where the first term measures the current price-cost margin, and the second term captures the value of the customer base.

Let $g_t \equiv c_t/s_{t-1} = (s_t/s_{t-1} - \rho)/(1 - \rho)$ and define the growth-adjusted discount factor $\tilde{\beta}_{t,s+1}$ as

$$\tilde{\beta}_{t,s+1} \equiv m_{s,s+1}g_{s+1} \times \prod_{j=1}^{s-t}\left[\rho + \theta(1 - \eta)(1 - \rho)g_{t+j}\right]m_{t+j-1,t+j}.$$

By iterating equation (15) forward, one can solve for the marginal value of an increase in the customer base—the term $\mathbb{E}_t^a[\lambda_t]/\mathbb{E}_t^a[\xi_{it}]$—as the growth-adjusted present value of marginal profits. Substituting the resulting expression into equation (23) then yields the value of marginal sales:

$$\frac{\mathbb{E}_t^a[\nu_{it}]}{\mathbb{E}_t^a[\xi_{it}]} = \frac{\tilde{\mu}_t - 1}{\tilde{\mu}_t} + \chi\mathbb{E}_t\left[\sum_{s=t+1}^{\infty}\tilde{\beta}_{t,s}\frac{\mathbb{E}_s^a[\xi_{is}]}{\mathbb{E}_t^a[\xi_{it}]}\left(\frac{\tilde{\mu}_s - 1}{\tilde{\mu}_s}\right)\right], \tag{24}$$

where $\chi = (1 - \rho)\theta(1 - \eta) > 0$ if $\theta < 0$ and $\eta > 1$.

In a symmetric price equilibrium, equation (16) implies $\mathbb{E}_t^a[\nu_{it}]/\mathbb{E}_t^a[\xi_{it}] = 1/\eta$. With customer markets, the markup is time-varying and balances future expected marginal costs against future expected growth opportunities. The internal liquidity condition of the firm—as summarized by the

23

sequence of $\mathbb{E}_s^a[\xi_{is}]$, $s = t, \ldots, \infty$—determines the weight that the firm places on current versus future profits when determining the expected price trajectory for its product. If today's liquidity premium outweighs the future liquidity premia, the firm places a greater weight on current profits relative to future profits and, as a result, sets a higher current markup.

3.4 Nominal Price Rigidities and the Phillips Curve

To allow for nominal rigidities, we follow Rotemberg (1982) and assume that firms face quadratic adjustment costs when changing nominal prices:

$$\frac{\gamma_p}{2}\left(\frac{P_{it}}{P_{i,t-1}} - \bar{\pi}\right)^2 c_t = \frac{\gamma_p}{2}\left(\pi_t \frac{p_{it}}{p_{i,t-1}} - \bar{\pi}\right)^2 c_t; \quad \gamma_p > 0.$$

As shown in Appendix B.2, the first-order condition governing the optimal choice of relative prices (equation 16) imply the following local inflation dynamics:

$$\hat{\pi}_t = \frac{1}{\gamma_p}(\hat{\xi}_t - \hat{\nu}_t) + \beta \mathbb{E}_t[\hat{\pi}_{t+1}], \tag{25}$$

where $\hat{\xi}_t$ and $\hat{\nu}_t$ denote the log-deviations of $\mathbb{E}_t^a[\xi_{it}]$ and $\mathbb{E}_t^a[\nu_{it}]$, respectively. In the absence of nominal rigidities, $\hat{\pi}_t = 0$ and consistent with equation (16), prices are set so that $\hat{\xi}_t = \hat{\nu}_t$. With nominal rigidities, equation (25) implies that given inflation expectations, the current inflation rate is determined by the expected shadow value of internal funds ($\mathbb{E}_t^a[\xi_{it}]$) relative to that of marginal sales ($\mathbb{E}_t^a[\nu_{it}]$).

To highlight the relationship between the model's structural parameters and inflation dynamics, we can log-linearize equation (24) and substitute the result in equation (25). These steps yield the following expression for the Phillips curve:

$$\hat{\pi}_t = -\frac{\omega(\eta - 1)}{\gamma_p}\left[\hat{\mu}_t + \mathbb{E}_t \sum_{s=t}^{\infty} \chi \tilde{\delta}^{s-t+1} \hat{\mu}_{s+1}\right] + \beta \mathbb{E}_t[\hat{\pi}_{t+1}]$$
$$+ \frac{1}{\gamma_p}[\eta - \omega(\eta - 1)] \mathbb{E}_t \sum_{s=t}^{\infty} \chi \tilde{\delta}^{s-t+1}\left[(\hat{\xi}_t - \hat{\xi}_{s+1}) - \hat{\beta}_{t,s+1}\right], \tag{26}$$

where $\omega = 1 - \beta\theta(1-\rho)/(1-\rho\beta)$, $\tilde{\delta} = \beta[\rho + \theta(1-\eta)(1-\rho)]$, $\hat{\mu}_t$ is the log-deviation of the financially adjusted markup $\tilde{\mu}_t$, and $\hat{\beta}_{t,s+1}$ is the log-deviation of the growth-adjusted discount factor $\tilde{\beta}_{t,s+1}$. Note that in the absence of external habit (that is, $\theta = 0$), $\omega = 1$ and $\chi = 0$, and we obtain the standard New Keynesian Phillips curve: $\hat{\pi}_t = -\hat{\mu}_t + \beta \mathbb{E}_t[\hat{\pi}_{t+1}]$; in that case, current inflation is equal to the present discounted value of expected future marginal cost (that is, the inverse of the markup).

With external habit but no financial distortions (that is, $\theta < 0$ and $\varphi_t = 0$), all terms involving $\hat{\xi}_t - \hat{\xi}_{s+1}$ in the second line of equation (26) drop out. However, with customer habits, $\chi > 0$, and there are two offsetting effects of demand-driven movements in output on current inflation conditional on expected future inflation. First, the present value of future markups directly enters the Phillips curve and implies that current inflation responds to future marginal cost, conditional on the next period's expected inflation. This term increases the sensitivity of current inflation to future fluctuations in output. Second, the term $\hat{\beta}_{t,s+1}$ captures the capitalized growth rate of the customer base and thus measures the present value of the marginal benefit from expanding the customer base today. According to equation (26), when the firm expects a greater benefit from the future customer base, it is more willing to lower the current price in order to build its customer base. This term thus reduces the sensitivity of current inflation to future output movements. Because these two effects offset each other, customer markets may lead to more or less responsiveness of inflation to output fluctuations.

Frictions in financial markets also have two effects on inflation dynamics. First, the markup must be adjusted for the distortions that create a cost channel. Under reasonable calibrations, this adjustment reduces the countercyclicality of the markup and attenuates the response of inflation to output fluctuations—this adjustment occurs regardless of whether we allow for customer habits. Second, customer habits imply that the firm takes into account the future customer base when setting its current price. In this case, financial distortions influence the effective discount factor captured by the shadow value of dividends today relative to the future—the term $\hat{\xi}_t - \hat{\xi}_{s+1}$. In practice, however, the effect of the cost channel is small, and the primary mechanism through which financial market frictions affect inflation is by altering the discount factor associated with how the firm values the benefits of the future customer base.

Faced with both a sticky customer base and costly external finance, firms are confronted with a fundamental tradeoff between current profits and the longer-run maximization of their market share, which is reflected in the term $(\hat{\xi}_t - \hat{\xi}_{s+1}) - \hat{\beta}_{t,s+1}$. Maintaining their market share requires firms to post low current prices. However, firms may be forced to deviate from this strategy, provided that their current internal liquidity position—as summarized by $\hat{\xi}_t$—is sufficiently weak relative to their future liquidity position $\hat{\xi}_{s+1}$. In that case, firms may raise their current prices in response to an adverse demand shock in order to avoid costly external financing, a pricing strategy that resembles a myopic optimization of current profits.[20]

3.5 Closing the Model

We assume that equity issuance costs are paid out to households and hence do not affect the aggregate resource constraint. Costs incurred when firms change nominal prices are similarly returned to households in a lump-sum manner. As detailed in Appendix B.1, the household's optimal

---

[20]The fundamental tradeoff between current cashflows and future market shares relies on the parameter restriction $\eta - \omega(\eta - 1) > 0$. Otherwise, firms in strong financial condition may *increase* their current prices in order to *increase* their long-run market shares. As long as θ, ρ, and η are chosen such that the steady-state marginal profit is strictly positive, we can exclude such pathological cases.

consumption-savings decision then implies that the stochastic discount factor $m_{t,t+1}$ satisfies

$$m_{t,t+1} = \beta \frac{U_x(x_{t+1} - \psi_{t+1}, h_{t+1})}{U_x(x_t - \psi_t, h_t)} \frac{s_{t-1}^\theta}{s_t^\theta}. \tag{27}$$

Letting r_t denote the ex ante nominal interest rate, then the Fisher equation may be expressed as

$$1 = \mathbb{E}_t \left[m_{t,t+1} \left(\frac{1 + r_t}{1 + \pi_{t+1}} \right) \right].$$

The efficiency condition governing the household's consumption-leisure choice is given by:[21]

$$\frac{w_t}{\tilde{p}_t} = -\frac{U_h(x_t - \psi_t, h_t)}{U_x(x_t - \psi_t, h_t)}. \tag{28}$$

The endogenous aggregate state variable s_t evolves according to $s_t = \rho s_{t-1} + (1 - \rho)c_t$, where, from the demand curve, the aggregate consumption index $x_t = c_t / s_t^\theta$.

The supply side of the model is then summarized by the markup equation (22), equation (24) governing the valuation of marginal sales, and the Phillips curve (26), along with the production function that determines labor demand, according to

$$h_t = \left[\frac{c_t + \phi}{\exp\left[0.5\alpha(1 + \alpha)\sigma^2 \right]} \right]^{\frac{1}{\alpha}}, \tag{29}$$

where the term in the denominator follows from the integration over the distribution of idiosyncratic technology shocks.[22]

The model also features a monetary authority that sets the nominal interest rate r_t using a Taylor-type rule that responds to inflation and output gaps:

$$r_t = (1 + r_{t-1})^{\tau_r} \left[(1 + \bar{r}) \left(\frac{\pi_t}{\pi^*} \right)^{\tau_\pi} \left(\frac{y_t}{y_t^*} \right)^{\tau_y} \right]^{1 - \tau_r} - 1. \tag{30}$$

The rule also allows for policy inertia, as reflected in letting $0 < \tau_r < 1$. In our baseline calibration of the model, we set $\tau_y = 0$, implying that monetary authorities respond only to inflation.

3.6 Model Calibration

A period in the model equals one quarter. Accordingly, the time discounting factor $\beta = 0.99$. Following Ravn et al. (2006), we set the deep habit parameter θ equal to -0.8. To highlight the

---

[21]In the numerical implementation of the model, we also assume convex adjustment costs for nominal wages (parametrized by γ_w) by introducing market power associated with differentiated labor; for expositional purposes, we omit those details.

[22]The adjusted markup $\tilde{\mu}_t$ and the expected external financing cost $\mathbb{E}_t^a[\xi_{it}]$ are static functions of aggregate variables. After substituting out for these variables, the model adds two dynamic equations—a backward-looking equation for the endogenous stock of habit s_t and the forward-looking valuation equation for $\mathbb{E}_t^a[\nu_{it}]/\mathbb{E}_t^a[\xi_{it}]$—to the otherwise standard three-equation log-linearized New Keynesian model.

firms' incentive to compete for market share, we also choose a fairly persistent habit formation process by assuming that only 5 percent of the habit stock is depreciated in a quarter (that is, the parameter ρ in equation (6) is set to 0.95).[23] The CRRA parameter in the household's utility function is then set equal to 1, given that the deep habit specification provides a strong motive to smooth consumption. We set the elasticity of labor supply equal to 5.

The elasticity of substitution across varieties of differentiated goods is a key parameter in the customer-markets model—smaller the degree of substitutability, greater is the firm's market power, and greater is its incentive to invest in customer base. Broda and Weinstein (2006) provide a set of estimates for the elasticity of substitution for the U.S. economy. According to their post-1990 data, the median value of the elasticity of substitution for differentiated goods at 2.1. Because this is a product category that is most relevant for the deep habits model, we set $\eta = 2.0$.

Another important parameter is the fixed operating cost ϕ, the value of which is determined jointly with the returns-to-scale parameter α. Specifically, we set α first and then choose ϕ so that the dividend-payout ratio (relative to income) hits the post-WWII mean value of about 2.5 percent. In our calibration, $\alpha = 0.8$, which then implies $\phi = 0.3$.[24] It is worth noting that in the model, decreasing returns to scale enhance the link between financial frictions and the firms' pricing decisions. Given the values of $\alpha = 0.8$, $\phi = 0.3$, and $\eta = 2.0$, the average gross markup in our model is equal to 1.19.

Following Cooley and Quadrini (2001), we calibrate the degree of financial market frictions—the equity dilution costs—by setting $\varphi_t = \bar{\varphi} = 0.3$. When analyzing the macroeconomic implications of financial disturbances—which we model as exogenous shocks to the time-varying equity dilution costs—we set the persistence of the financial shock to 0.9. To abstract from the differences in the persistence of different aggregate disturbances, the AR(1) parameter for the demand shock ψ_t is also set equal to 0.9. The volatility of the idiosyncratic technology shock is calibrated at 0.05 (20 percent at an annual rate), implying a moderate amount of idiosyncratic uncertainty. With the fixed operating cost calibrated as described above, the combination of $\sigma = 0.05$ and $\bar{\varphi} = 0.3$ yields an annualized expected premium on external funds of about 13 percent (that is, $\mathbb{E}^a[\xi_i] = 1.127$). In our crisis experiment, a simulation exercise that imposes an extreme degree of financial distortions, we let $\bar{\varphi} = 0.5$, in which case, the premium on external funds jumps to 20 percent.

For the parameters related to nominal rigidities, we set the adjustment costs of nominal prices $\gamma_p = 10.0$ and wages $\gamma_w = 30.0$. These values are within the range of point estimates of 14.5 and 41.0 in Ravn et al. (2006), who show that deep habits substantially enhance the persistence of inflation, without the reliance on an implausibly large amount of stickiness in nominal prices. Finally, we set the interest rate smoothing coefficient τ_r in the policy rule (30) at a conventional level of 0.75, and τ_π, the coefficient on the inflation gap, at 1.5, values in line with those used in the New Keynesian literature.

---

[23]Our calibration of the external habit process is only marginally more persistent than that of Ravn et al. (2006).

[24]This degree of returns to scale is common in the empirical literature that relies on firm-level data (see Hennessy and Whited, 2007). Model's dynamics are not substantially affected by varying this parameter between 0.8 and 1.0.

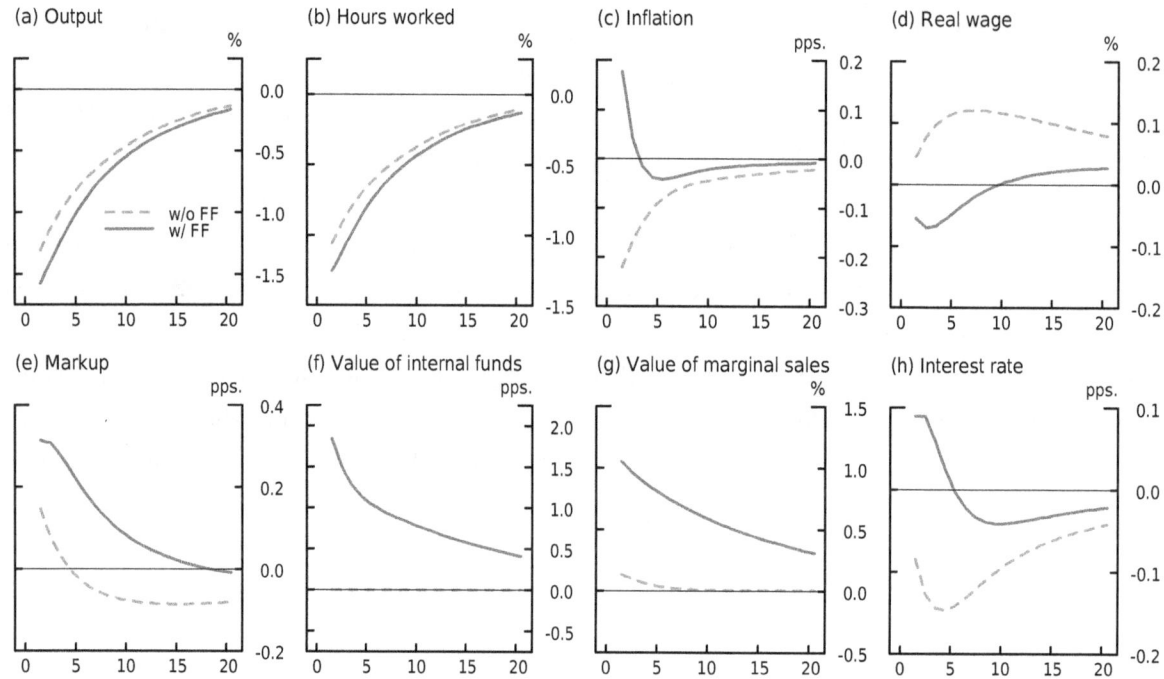

NOTE: The panels of the figure depict the model-implied responses of selected variables to a negative demand shock of 1 standard deviation: w/ FF = responses implied by a model with financial frictions, with the degree of financial frictions calibrated to a crisis situation ($\bar{\varphi} = 0.5$); and w/o FF = responses implied by a model without financial frictions ($\bar{\varphi} = 0$).

4 Model Simulations: Homogeneous Firms

To study the implications of customer markets and financial frictions for inflation and output dynamics, this section reports results from two experiments. First, we consider a persistent decline in demand in an environment where external finance is highly costly—a crisis situation. We then consider an exogenous temporary increase in the cost of external finance—a financial shock.

4.1 Financial Crisis and Inflation Dynamics

To implement a financial crisis in the model, we set $\varphi_t = \bar{\varphi} = 0.5$, which implies an external finance premium of 20 percent (annualized). Such a high expected cost of external funds strikes us as plausible in the latter part of 2008, a period during which the commercial paper market froze, corporate bond credit spreads blew out, equity prices tanked, and asset price volatility skyrocketed. The solid lines in Figure 6 show the macroeconomic impact of an adverse demand shock under such extreme circumstances. To highlight the role of financial frictions, the dotted lines show the effect of the same shock in the economy with perfect capital markets.

In the absence of financial distortions, the negative demand shock leads a drop in real output and a decline in inflation. The comparison of responses in panel (a) reveals that financial frictions amplify the response of output to a demand shock, a result consistent with the standard financial accelerator mechanism. Although differences in output dynamics are fairly modest, the initial response of inflation differs substantially across the two models. In particular, in the model with financial frictions, inflation rises rather than falls. The explanation for this striking difference can be found in panels (e)–(f). Our timing assumptions imply that firms are aware that the economy has been hit by a demand shock before making their pricing decisions. In the presence of financial distortions, this reduces the firms' expected cashflows and increases the probability that they will require costly external finance. As a result, the shadow value of internal funds jumps almost 200 basis points upon the impact of the shock (panel (f)). To protect themselves against the idiosyncratic tail event in which the ex post cashflows are negative and they must raise costly external finance, firms significantly boost their markups relative to the model without financial frictions (panel (e)).

The severity of financial frictions in a crisis situation causes the value of internal funds and the value of marginal sales to move in tandem (panels (f) and (g)). Because cashflows are discounted using internal valuations, financial distortions create a direct link between the two valuations, which does not exist in an economy with frictionless financial markets. Note that in both models, the demand shock leads to a sharp initial increase in the markup (panel (e)). Financial frictions, however, substantially amplify the countercyclical behavior of markups—the increase in the markup in the model with financial distortions is double that implied by the model without such distortions. Moreover, in an economy with financial frictions, the markup remains elevated for quite some time after the initial impact of the shock, while in the frictionless case, the high initial markup is offset by low future markups. As highlighted in panels (f) and (g), the driving force behind the strong countercyclical nature of markups in the presence of financial distortions is the deterioration in the firms' internal liquidity positions, which causes firms to increase markups in an effort to stabilize near-term profits in the face of falling demand.

Figure 7 considers the same experiment, but in an environment without nominal (price and wage) rigidities. The negative demand shock again causes a drop in output and hours worked and, in the model with financial frictions, an increase in the value of internal funds. In the absence of financial distortions, the markup is not affected by the demand shock upon impact but then declines gradually and remains persistently below steady state. Thus, in the absence of nominal rigidities and financial distortions, the markup is strongly procyclical in response to demand shocks in this version of the deep habits model. Adding sticky prices alone to the model imparts at best only a modest degree of countercyclicality to the markup. However, with the addition of financial frictions, the markup becomes strongly countercyclical, as firms seek to increase current profits to overcome the liquidity squeeze.

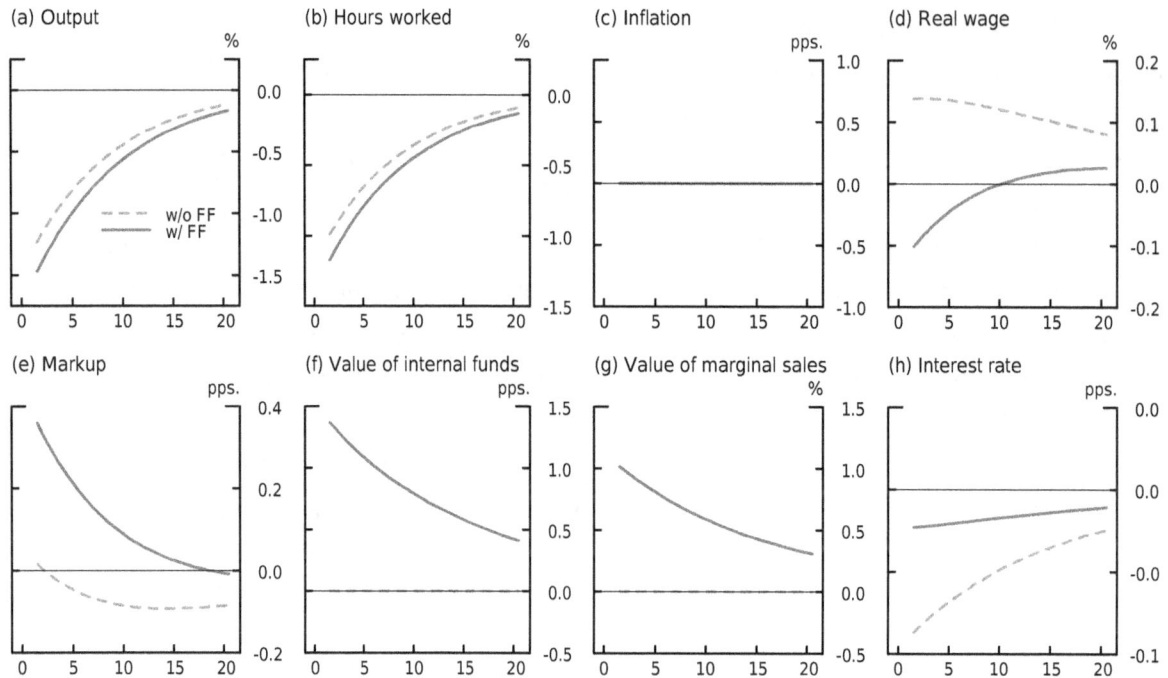

NOTE: The panels of the figure depict the model-implied responses of selected variables to a negative demand shock of 1 standard deviation: w/ FF = responses implied by a model with financial frictions, with the degree of financial frictions calibrated to a crisis situation ($\bar{\varphi} = 0.5$); and w/o FF = responses implied by a model without financial frictions ($\bar{\varphi} = 0$).

4.2 Financial Shocks and Inflation Dynamics

We now consider the macroeconomic implications of financial shocks. That is, rather than considering a crisis situation in which it is extremely costly to raise outside equity, we introduce financial distress in the model by considering a disturbance that temporarily boosts the cost of external finance. As discussed above, we implement this idea by assuming that the equity issuance cost parameter φ_t follows a process of the form:

$$\varphi_t = \bar{\varphi} f_t; \quad \log f_t = 0.90 \times \log f_{t-1} + \epsilon_t^f.$$

Using this framework, we then analyze the effects of a financial shock ϵ_t^f that increases equity dilution costs 25 percent from their steady-state level upon impact.

Under our baseline calibration ($\bar{\varphi} = 0.3$), this financial shock boosts the level of equity dilution costs from 0.3 to 0.375 upon impact, a degree of financial distortions that is significantly below that assumed in the crisis situation. The solid lines in Figure 8 show the macroeconomic implications of such temporary increase in financial distress. To help highlight the importance of customer markets in our model, the dotted lines show the corresponding responses of the economy facing the same

Figure 8: The Impact of a Financial Shock
(*With Nominal Rigidities*)

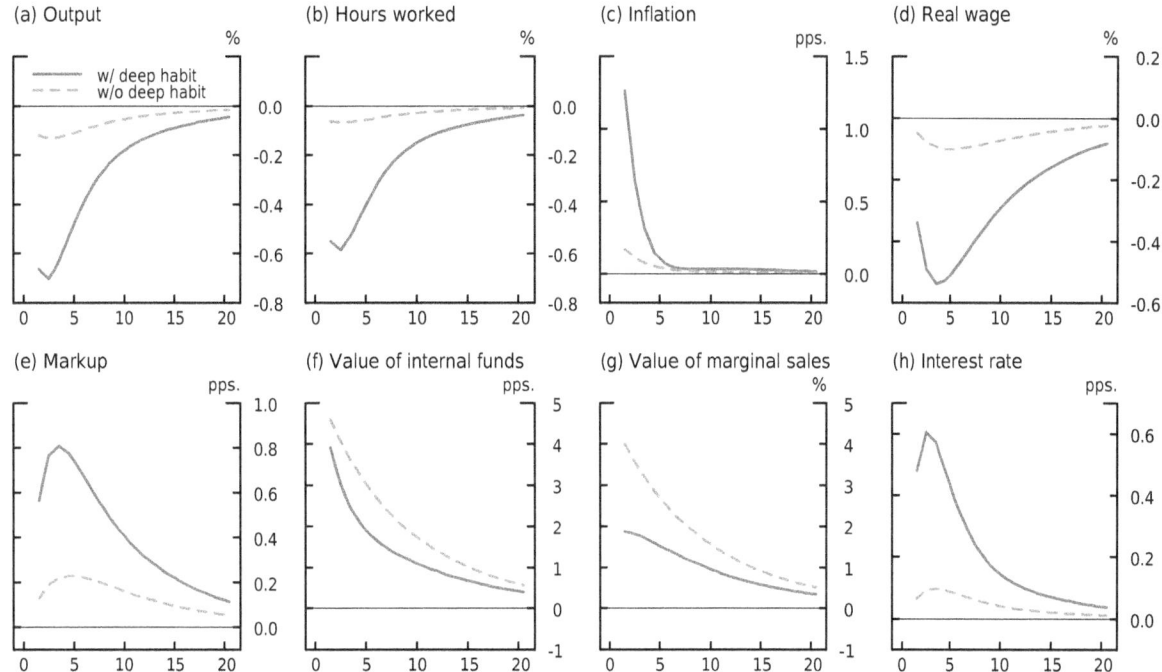

NOTE: The panels of the figure depict the model-implied responses of selected variables to a temporary increase in the time-varying equity dilution cost parameter φ_t: w/ deep habit = responses implied by a model with deep habits ($\theta = -0.8$); and w/o deep habit = responses implied by a model without deep habits ($\theta = 0$).

degree of financial distress but no customer markets—this corresponds to a financial shock in a model that incorporates only the cost-channel mechanism.

According to panels (a) and (b), the temporary increase in external financing costs has large effects on economic activity in an environment where financial distortions interact with customer markets: The immediate decline in both output and hours worked in response to a contractionary demand shock is larger by a factor of ten, compared with an economy that features only financial market frictions and thus only allows for the traditional cost channel. The response of inflation is also amplified substantially when financial frictions interact with customer markets, compared with the case where only the cost channel is present. In effect, a temporary deterioration in the firms' internal liquidity positions shrinks the financial capacity of the economy, a development that directly shifts the Phillips curve upward.

Panels (e), (f), and (g) show the essential mechanism at work. When the economy is hit by a financial shock, the markup, the shadow value of internal funds, and the value of marginal sales all increase sharply. In the absence of customer markets, the rise in the value of internal funds is almost entirely offset by the increase in the value of an additional sale, implying very little change in the

Figure 9: Impact of a Demand Shock During Financial Crisis
(*Alternative Monetary Policy Rules*)

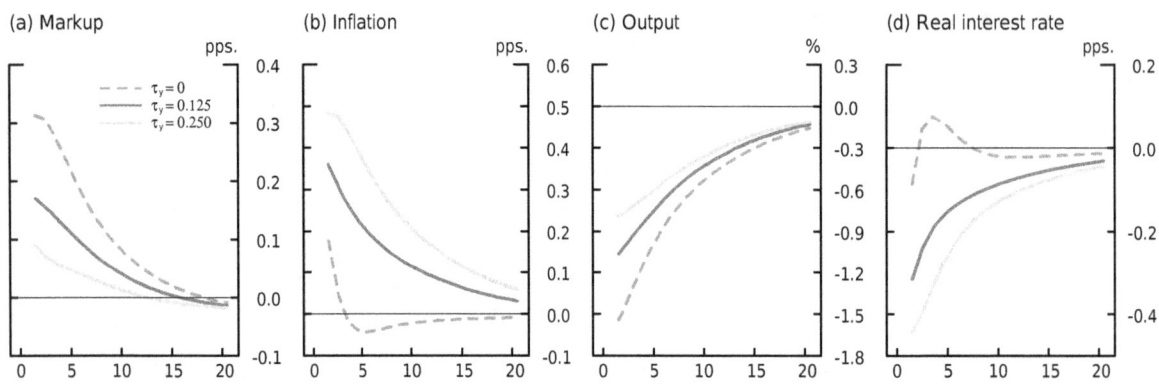

(a) Markup   (b) Inflation   (c) Output   (d) Real interest rate

NOTE: The panels of the figure depict the model-implied responses of selected variables to a negative demand shock of 1 standard deviation for different values of an output gap coefficient τ_y in the monetary policy rule. All responses are based on the model featuring nominal rigidities and financial frictions, with the level of financial frictions calibrated to a crisis situation ($\bar{\varphi} = 0.5$).

financially adjusted markup (see equation 22).[25] With customer markets, however, the financial shock enters independently as a cost-push factor in the Phillips curve because firms recognize that they may trade off current cashflows for future market share and, as a result, are willing to increase markups.

As output falls, the habit stock declines, generating a further deterioration in the firms' liquidity positions. In effect, customer capital acts as a form of financial capital at times when internal liquidity is scarce. When habit stocks and hence output are low relative to fixed operating costs, firms are more likely to require costly external finance. Thus, the presence of customer markets generates both greater amplification and greater persistence relative to the model featuring only the standard cost-channel mechanism. As shown in panel (h), the rise in inflation also prompts an increase in the nominal interest rate in the customer markets model. Although the interest rate rule used by the monetary authorities puts zero weight on the output gap, the nominal interest rate increases by considerably less than inflation because of the interest-rate smoothing motive. This causes a sharp decline in the real interest rate. The model with customer markets, therefore, provides substantial amplification in spite of a strongly countercyclical monetary policy.

4.3 Monetary Policy Implications

According to the simulations shown in Figures 6 and 8, output falls while inflation rises in response to a contractionary demand shock or an adverse financial disturbance. These macroeconomic dynamics stand in sharp contrast to those implied by either standard New Keynesian models or financial accelerator models that work through investment demand—in both of these frameworks, output and inflation exhibit strong positive comovement in response to such shocks. Indeed, this positive comovement is at the heart of the so-called divine coincidence of monetary policy, whereby monetary authorities—by lowering nominal interest rates—can simultaneously stabilize both output and inflation and thus eliminate any concern of an active tradeoff for monetary policy.

To explore implications of our model for monetary policy, we re-consider the crisis experiment shown in Figure 6 by allowing monetary authorities to respond to inflation and output. Figure 9 reports the results of this simulation for the output gap coefficient τ_y equal to 0.125 and 0.25; for comparison purposes, the figure also shows the responses from the original exercise in which $\tau_y = 0$, that is, the central bank is concerned only about inflation.[26] As evidenced by the differences in the impulse responses, increasing the coefficient on the output gap successfully stabilizes output but comes at the very obvious cost of destabilizing inflation. In our model, therefore, the divine coincidence fails to hold, and there exists a meaningful tradeoff between output and inflation stabilization in response to demand and financial shocks.[27]

5   Model Simulations: Heterogeneous Firms

In the above simulations, we exploited the notion of symmetric equilibrium, according to which all firms in the model chose the same price. We now consider our full model with firm heterogeneity, which generates a nondegenerate equilibrium distribution of prices across firms in the economy. Allowing for firm heterogeneity highlights an important aspect of the interaction between customer markets and financial market frictions in periods of financial distress. In a crisis situation, financially strong firms—in response to an adverse demand shock—attempt to drive out their weaker competitors by undercutting their prices. This "price war" creates an aggregate demand externality, whereby significant heterogeneity in financial conditions across firms may lead to a greater contraction in output relative to a situation in which firms are more uniformly constrained in their

---

[25]The increase in the value of marginal sales in the model with customer markets is significantly attenuated in comparison with the model without customer markets. This differential response reflects the fact that in the former model, the value of marginal sales is less responsive to shocks because it captures the entire present discounted value of the customer base. Nonetheless, the markup, and thus inflation dynamics, are determined by the gap between the value of internal funds and the value of marginal sales, which in the customer markets model widens considerably in response to a financial shock.

[26]In all three of these cases, the coefficient on the inflation gap in the policy rule $\tau_\pi = 1.5$, while the degree of interest rate smoothing $\tau_r = 0.75$.

[27]In addition to examining model sensitivity to different monetary policy rules, we have also considered the effect of a binding zero lower bound on nominal interest rates. In the model with customer markets and financial frictions, output declines leads to upward inflationary pressure. As a result, real interest rates fall by less and the amount of time spent at the zero lower bound is curtailed. Hence, the effects of a binding zero lower bound are substantially mitigated relative to a model with frictionless financial markets.

access to external finance.

5.1 Heterogeneous Operating Costs

To introduce heterogeneity in the model, we modify the production technology in equation (9), according to

$$y_{it} = \left(\frac{A_t}{a_{it}} h_{it}\right)^{\alpha} - \phi_i, \tag{31}$$

where ϕ_i denotes fixed operating costs of firm i. These costs can take on one of N-values from a set $\{\phi_1, \ldots, \phi_N\}$, where $0 \leq \phi_1 < \cdots < \phi_N$. The measure of firms at the level of operating efficiency ϕ_k is denoted by Ξ_k, where $\sum_{k=1}^{N} \Xi_k = 1$. Lastly, we also assume that all firms face the same distribution of the idiosyncratic technology shock a_{it} (that is, $\log a_{it} \sim N(-0.5\sigma^2, \sigma^2)$).

As shown in Appendix B.1, the introduction of heterogeneous operating costs implies that the external financing trigger is specific to each sector k, with $d\mathbb{E}_t^a[\xi_{it}|\phi_k]/d\phi_k > 0$. Thus, the lower the level of operating efficiency, the greater is the likelihood that the firm will have difficulties meeting its liquidity needs using only internally generated funds. In other words, all firms in a sector characterized by low operating efficiency face higher expected external financing costs and thus are considered to be financially "weak."

Within this framework, we again consider a symmetric equilibrium, in which all firms with a given level of operating efficiency choose the same price and production scale. The derivation of firm-specific prices, financing costs, labor inputs, and output decisions is analogous to the homogeneous model. In particular, firm-specific inflation rates evolve according to a sector-specific Phillips curve. Note that although all firms with the same ϕ_k choose the same price level, sectoral heterogeneity in fixed operating costs generates dispersion of prices across firms. Aggregate quantities are then obtained in a standard manner. Specifically, the aggregate inflation rate can be expressed as a weighted average of sectoral inflation rates:

$$\pi_t = \left[\sum_{k=1}^{N} \Xi_k (p_{k,t-1}\pi_{kt})^{1-\eta}\right]^{\frac{1}{1-\eta}}, \tag{32}$$

where $\pi_{kt} \equiv P_{kt}/P_{k,t-1}$ and $p_{kt} \equiv P_{kt}/P_t$ denote sector-specific inflation rates and relative prices, respectively.

5.2 Countercyclical Dispersion of Inflation Rates

For maximum intuition, we consider only two sectors in our numerical simulations. The first sector consists of financially "strong" firms, which are characterized by having $\phi_1 = 0$. The second sector is made up of financially "weak" firms, distinguished by having $\phi_2 = 0.3$, the value used in our baseline calibration. For simplicity, we assume that the two sectors are of equal sizes—that is, $\Xi_1 = \Xi_2 = 0.5$. Within this setup, we seek to answer the following question: In periods of financial turmoil, do financially strong firms slash their prices to drive out their weaker competitors? To answer

34

Figure 10: The Impact of a Financial Shock
(*Heterogeneous Firms*)

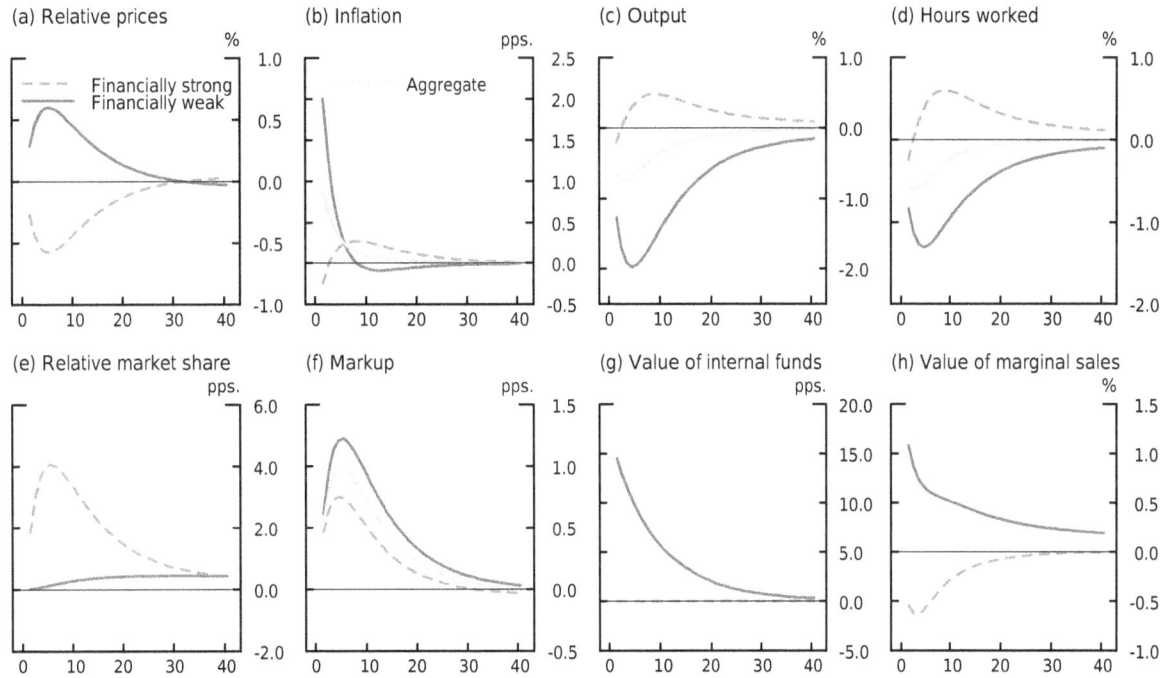

NOTE: The panels of the figure depict the model-implied responses of selected variables to a temporary increase in the time-varying equity dilution cost parameter φ_t. The sector consisting of financially strong firms is defined by the operating efficiency level $\phi_1 = 0$, whereas the sector consisting of financially weak firms has the operating efficiency level $\phi_2 = 0.3$. The aggregate responses are computed under the assumption that the two sectors are of equal sizes.

this question, we perturb the model economy with a financial shock, which, as in subsection 4.2, corresponds to a temporary increase in equity dilution costs from their normal level ($\bar{\varphi} = 0.3$).

The solid line in panel (a) of Figure 10 shows the response of relative prices ($p_{kt} = P_{kt}/P_t$) for financially weak firms, whereas the dashed line depicts the corresponding response of their financially strong counterparts. In response to an adverse financial shock, financially healthy firms cut their prices—behavior consistent with the concurrent decline in aggregate output—while the financially vulnerable firms actually increase their prices in an effort to avoid costly external financing. Panel (b) translates this difference in the price-setting behavior into the sector-specific inflation rates ($\pi_{kt} = P_{kt}/P_{k,t-1}$). Clearly evident is the countercyclical behavior of the dispersion in inflation rates, a result consistent with that documented by Vavra (2014).[28]

Panel (c) shows the dynamics of output. As a result of "winning" the price war, financially strong firms gradually expand output in order to satisfy the growing demand engendered by the relative price cut. Financially weak firms, by contrast, slash production, a move that causes the

---

[28]In our case, the countercyclical dispersion in inflation rates arises endogenously in response to the differences in financial conditions across firms, whereas Vavra (2014) relies on an exogenous second-moment (that is, uncertainty) shock that is calibrated countercyclically.

aggregate output and hour worked to decline moderately. Again, the dispersion in output and hours worked at the micro level is generated endogenously by the distortions in financial markets.

The dynamics of the relative market shares of the two sectors are shown in panel (e). Consistent with their aggressive pricing behavior, financially healthy firms significantly expand their market share during the economic downturn. Because of the deep-habit preferences, the customer base of financially strong firms expands only gradually, though the expansion is quite persistent. Moreover, the customers that switched products during the downturn form a loyal group, as a substantial part of them stays with the new products, even after the relative prices of the goods produced in the two sectors return to their respective steady-state levels. For example, after 20 quarters, the relative prices charged by financially strong firms are for all practical purposes back to their normal level, but their relative market share remains elevated, which highlights the primary reason why undercutting competitors' prices can be such a profitable investment.

5.3   The Paradox of Financial Strength

The above example highlights the willingness of firms with strong balance sheets to undercut prices of firms with weak balance sheets during economic downturns. We now consider whether firms with ample financial capacity can slash their prices so aggressively that they drive out the financially weaker firms to such an extent so as to generate a sizable drop in aggregate output. Such a scenario can be implemented in several different ways. One way is to make the contribution of the habit to the final demand more important and more persistent by choosing higher values for θ and ρ. Alternatively, we can reduce the price elasticity of demand by lowering η. We follow the first approach and set $\theta = -0.85$ and $\rho = 0.985$ compared to baseline values of $\theta = -0.8$ and $\rho = 0.9$.

Using this new calibration, we consider two model specifications, distinguished only by the degree of firm heterogeneity. In the first specification (Case I), we assume that $\phi_1 = 0.8\phi_2$ and $\phi_2 = 0.3$; the second specification (Case II) has $\phi_1 = 0$ and $\phi_2 = 0.3$. In both cases, the two sectors are of the same size. Note that although the first model features a greater proportion of financially weak firms compared with the second model, there is considerably less heterogeneity in financial conditions across firms in that case. The dynamics of relative prices and output in response to our standard financial shock are depicted in Figure 11.

The paradox of financial strength can be seen from the fact that a financially more fragile economy (Case I) experiences a noticeably less severe decline in aggregate output in response to an adverse financial shock, compared with the economy that overall has greater financial capacity but more pronounced heterogeneity in the relative strength of the firms' balance sheets (Case II). As shown in the top two panels, this difference reflects the inability of financially strong firms in the first model to slash prices as aggressively as their counterparts in the second model: The price cut by financially strong firms in the first case is less than one-half of that implemented by the financially strong firms in the second case. According to the bottom two panels, the aggressive pricing strategy of financially healthy firms in the case with greater heterogeneity in financial conditions is a Pyrrhic victory because it drives down the output of financially weak firms to such

36

Figure 11: The Paradox of Financial Strength
(*Heterogeneous Firms*)

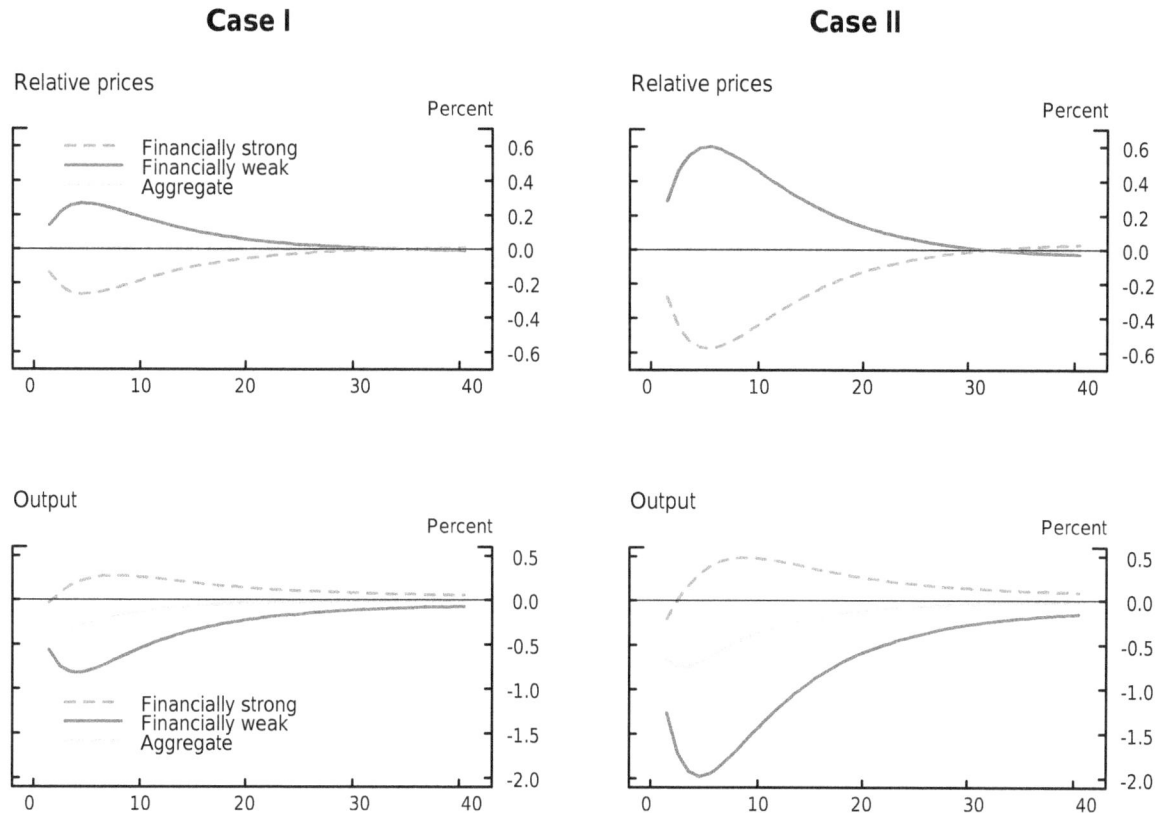

NOTE: The panels of the figure depict the model-implied responses of selected variables to a temporary increase in the time-varying equity dilution cost parameter φ_t. Case I: model specification with $\phi_1 = 0.8\phi_2$, with $\phi_2 = 0.3$; and Case II: model specification with $\phi_1 = 0$ and $\phi_2 = 0.3$. In both cases, financially strong firms are in sector 1, which is characterized by the operating efficiency level ϕ_1; financially weak firms, in contrast, operate in sector 2 with the efficiency level ϕ_2. The aggregate responses are computed under the assumption that the two sectors are of equal sizes.

an extent that the economy experiences a significantly more severe economic slump than in the case with less heterogeneity but an overall greater degree of financial fragility.[29]

6 Conclusion

This paper analyzes inflation dynamics during the 2007–09 financial crisis through the lens of customer-markets theory, while dispensing with the assumption of frictionless financial markets. The theoretical exploration of this mechanism is motivated by new empirical evidence, which shows that firms with limited internal liquidity significantly increased their prices in 2008, a period char-

---

[29]This finding also suggests that macroeconomic stabilization policies aimed at providing liquidity support to financially vulnerable firms during periods of financial distress may offer an effective tool to avoid a severe deterioration in economic activity associated with credit cycles.

acterized by the widespread disruptions in credit markets and a sharp contraction in output. Their liquidity unconstrained counterparts, by contrast, cut prices, a move consistent with the standard pricing models. The differences in the price-setting behavior between these two types of firms are concentrated in nondurable goods manufacturing, a sector where firms' pricing decisions are more likely influenced by customer retention and acquisition considerations, the key features of customer markets.

To explore the macroeconomic implication of financial frictions in customer markets, we develop a general equilibrium model, in which monopolistically competitive firms face costly price adjustment and costly external finance, while setting prices to actively manage current versus future expected demand. In this environment, financial distortions create an incentive for firms to raise prices in response to adverse demand or financial shocks, a price-setting behavior reflecting the firms' reaction to preserve internal liquidity and avoid accessing costly external finance. In economic booms, by contrast, the competition for market shares mitigates the upward pressure on prices. The combination of financial frictions and customer markets thus strengthens the counter-cyclical behavior of markups and significantly attenuates the response of inflation to demand and financial shocks.

Allowing for differences in financial conditions across firms, model simulations show that firms with weak balance sheets raise prices relative to firms with strong balance sheets in response to adverse financial shocks. The price cuts by firms with strong balance sheets and the resulting gains in their market share lead to a further deterioration in the liquidity position of financially constrained firms, which amplifies the decline in aggregate output. Both empirical results and model simulations thus support the notion that in periods of widespread financial distress, the interaction of customer markets with financial frictions can significantly dampen the downward pressure on prices and account for the stabilization of inflation in the face of significant and long-lasting economic slack.

Combining customer markets theory with financial market frictions also has important implications for the conduct of monetary policy. In the absence of financial frictions, inflation and output exhibit strong comovement and reducing nominal interest rates successfully stabilizes inflation and output in response to negative demand or financial shocks. With financial distortions, however, adverse demand and financial shocks shift the Phillips curve upwards. As a result, the divine coincidence fails to hold, and monetary authorities face an active tradeoff between inflation and output stabilization in response to both demand and financial disturbances.

References

ANDERSON, E., E. NAKAMURA, D. SIMESTER, AND J. STEINSSON (2014): "Informational Rigidities and the Stickiness of Temporary Sales," Working Paper, Dept. of Economics, Columbia University.

ASPLUND, M., R. ERIKSSON, AND N. STRAND (2005): "Prices, Margins, and Liquidity Constraints: Swedish Newspapers 1990–1992," *Economica*, 72, 349–359.

BALL, L. M. AND S. MAZUMDER (2011): "Inflation Dynamics and the Great Recession," *Brookings Papers on Economic Activity*, 42, 337–405.

BARTH, M. J. AND V. A. RAMEY (2001): "The Cost Channel of Monetary Transmission," in *NBER Macroeconomics Annual*, ed. by B. S. Bernanke and K. Rogoff, Cambridge: The MIT Press, vol. 16, 199–249.

BASSETT, W. F., M. B. CHOSAK, J. C. DRISCOLL, AND E. ZAKRAJŠEK (2014): "Changes in Bank Lending Standards and the Macroeconomy," *Journal of Monetary Economics*, 62, 23–40.

BERNANKE, B. S., M. GERTLER, AND S. GILCHRIST (1999): "The Financial Accelerator in a Quantitative Business Cycle Framework," in *The Handbook of Macroeconomics*, ed. by J. B. Taylor and M. Woodford, Amsterdam: Elsevier Science B.V, 1341–1393.

BILS, M. (1989): "Pricing in a Customer Market," *Quarterly Journal of Economics*, 104, 699–718.

BILS, M. AND P. J. KLENOW (2004): "Some Evidence on the Importance of Sticky Prices," *Journal of Political Economy*, 112, 947–985.

BILS, M., P. J. KLENOW, AND B. A. MALIN (2013): "Testing for Keynesian Labor Demand," in *NBER Macroeconomics Annual*, National Bureau of Economic Research, Inc, vol. 27, 311–349.

BLINDER, A. S., E. D. CANETTI, D. E. LEBOW, AND J. B. RUUD (1998): *Asking About Prices: A New Approach to Understanding Price Stickiness*, New York: Russell Sage Foundation.

BRODA, C. AND D. E. WEINSTEIN (2006): "Globalization and the Gains from Variety," *Quarterly Journal of Economics*, 121, 541–585.

BRONNENBERG, B., J.-P. DUBE, AND M. GENTZKOW (2012): "The Evolution of Brand Preferences: Evidence From Consumer Migration," *American Economic Review*, 104, 2472–2508.

CAMPELLO, M., E. GIAMBONA, J. R. GRAHAM, AND C. R. HARVEY (2011): "Liquidity Management and Corporate Investment During a Financial Crisis," *Review of Financial Studies*, 24, 1944–1979.

CHEVALIER, J. A. AND D. S. SCHARFSTEIN (1996): "Capital-Market Imperfections and Countercylical Markups: Theory and Evidence," *American Economic Review*, 86, 703–725.

CHRISTIANO, L. J., M. S. EICHENBAUM, AND M. TRABANDT (2015): "Understanding the Great Recession," *American Economic Journal: Macroeconomics*, 7, 110–167.

COIBON, O. AND Y. GORODNICHENKO (2015): "Is The Phillips Curve Alive and Well After All? Inflation Expectations and the Missing Disinflation," *American Economic Journal: Macroeconomics*, 7, 197–232.

COOLEY, T. F. AND V. QUADRINI (2001): "Financial Markets and Firm Dynamics," *American Economic Review*, 91, 1286–1310.

DEL NEGRO, M., M. P. GIANNONI, AND F. SCHORFHEIDE (2015): "Inflation in the Great Recession and New Keynesian Models," *American Economic Journal: Macroeconomics*, 7, 168–196.

GOLDBERG, P. K. AND R. HELLERSTEIN (2009): "How Rigid are Producer Prices?" Staff Report No. 407, Federal Reserve Bank of New York.

GOPINATH, G. AND O. ITSKHOKI (2011): "In Search of Real Rigidities," in *NBER Macroconomics Annual*, ed. by D. Acemoglu and M. Woodford, Chicago: The University of Chicago Press, 261–309.

GORDON, R. J. (2013): "The Phillips Curve is Alive and Well: Inflation and the NAIRU During the Slow Recovery," NBER Working Paper No. 19390.

GOTTFRIES, N. (1991): "Customer Markets, Credit Market Imperfections and Real Price Rigidity," *Economica*, 58, 317–323.

GOURIO, F. AND L. RUDANKO (2011): "Customer Capital," NBER Working Paper No. 17191.

HALL, R. E. (2008): "General Equilibrium With Customer Relationships: A Dynamic Analysis of Rent-Seeking," Working Paper, Dept. of Economics, Stanford University.

——— (2011): "The Long Slump," *American Economic Review*, 101, 431–469.

HENNESSY, C. A. AND T. M. WHITED (2007): "How Costly is External Financing? Evidence From Structural Estimation," *Journal of Finance*, 62, 1705–1745.

KILEY, M. T. AND J. W. SIM (2012): "Intermediary Leverage, Macroeconomic Dynamics, and Macroprudential Policy," Working Paper, Federal Reserve Board of Governors.

KIMURA, T. (2013): "Why Do Prices Remain Stable in the Bubble and Bust Period?" *International Economic Journal*, 27, 157–177.

KING, R. G. AND M. W. WATSON (2012): "Inflation and Unit Labor Cost," *Journal of Money, Credit, and Banking*, 44, 111–149.

KLEMPERER, P. (1987): "Market With Customer Switching Costs," *Quarterly Journal of Economics*, 102, 375–394.

KRUEGER, A. B., J. CRAMER, AND D. CHO (2014): "Are the Long-Term Unemployed on the Margins of the Labor Market?" *Brookings Papers on Economic Activity*, 48, 229–298.

LINS, K. V., H. SERVAES, AND P. TUFANO (2010): "What Drives Corporate Liquidity? An International Survey of Cash Holdings and Lines of Credit," *Journal of Financial Economics*, 98, 160–176.

LUNDIN, M., N. GOTTFRIES, C. BUCHT, AND T. LINDSTRÖM (2009): "Price and Investment Dynamics: Theory and Plant-Level Data," *Journal of Money, Credit, and Banking*, 41, 907–934.

MONTERO, J. AND A. URTASUN (2014): "Price-Cost Markups in the Spanish Economy: A Microeconomic Perspective," Working Paper No. 1407, Bank of Spain.

NAKAMURA, E. AND J. STEINSSON (2008): "Five Facts about Prices: A Reevaluation of Menu Cost Models," *Quarterly Journal of Economics*, 123, 1415–1464.

——— (2011): "Price Setting in Forward-Looking Customer Markets," *Journal of Monetary Economics*, 58, 220–233.

PHELPS, E. S. AND S. G. WINTER (1970): "Optimal Price Policy Under Atomistic Competition," in *Microeconomic Foundations of Employment and Inflation Theory*, ed. by E. S. Phelps, New York: W. W. Norton & Co., 309–337.

RAVN, M. O., S. SCHMITT-GROHE, AND M. URIBE (2006): "Deep Habits," *Review of Economic Studies*, 73, 195–218.

ROTEMBERG, J. J. (1982): "Monopolistic Price Adjustment and Aggregate Output," *Review of Economic Studies*, 49, 517–531.

ROTEMBERG, J. J. AND M. WOODFORD (1991): "Markups and the Business Cycle," in *NBER Macroeconomics Annual*, ed. by O. J. Blanchard and S. Fischer, Cambridge: The MIT Press, 63–140.

SCHOENLE, R. (2010): "International Menu Costs and Price Dynamics," Working Paper, Dept. of Economics, Princeton University.

VAVRA, J. S. (2014): "Inflation Dynamics and Time-Varying Volatility: New Evidence and an Ss Interpretation," *Quarterly Journal of Economics*, 129, 215–258.

Appendices – For Online Publication

A   Data Appendix

A.1   Full PPI vs. Matched PPI–Compustat Samples

Compared with the full PPI sample, the matched PPI–Compustat panel is more heavily concentrated on the manufacturing sector (2-digit NAICS 31–33). More than 90 percent of goods in the matched PPI–Compustat data set are produced by manufacturing firms, compared with about 60 percent in the full PPI data set. Table A-1 compares the key cross-sectional price-change characteristics between the full PPI and matched PPI–Compustat data sets. In the first step, we calculate the *average* price-change characteristic for each good; in the case of good-level inflation, for example, we compute $\pi_{i,j,\cdot} = T_i^{-1} \sum_{t=1}^{T_i} \pi_{i,j,t}$, where T_i denotes the number of months that good i is in the sample. In the second step, we compute the summary statistics of the average good-specific price change characteristics for the two data sets.

An average establishment in the PPI–Compustat panel reports in an average month price information on 5.4 goods, whereas its counterpart in the full PPI panel does so for 4.3 goods. In addition, prices of goods produced by the former are, on average, sampled over a longer time period—51.2 months compared with 42.3 months. Despite these differences, the cross-sectional price change characteristics are very similar across the two samples. The price of an average good in the full PPI panel increases 0.15 percent per month, on average, over its lifetime in the sample, compared with 0.12 percent for an average good in the PPI–Compustat panel. Not surprisingly, the dispersion of average good-level inflation rates in the full PPI sample is noticeably higher than that in the matched PPI–Compustat sample, reflecting the fact that the former sample contains many goods with very volatile prices. In both data sets, the distributions of positive and negative price changes are also very comparable: The median of the average good-specific positive inflation rates is 5.2 percent for the full PPI sample and 4.8 percent for the matched PPI–Compustat sample; the corresponding medians of the average good-specific negative inflation rates are -4.8 percent and -4.4 percent, respectively.

On average, the probability with which prices of an average good are adjusted in the full PPI panel is 16 percent per month, compared with 18 percent per month for the PPI–Compustat panel; that is, an average good changes its price about every 6 months in both data sets. However, as evidenced by the associated standard deviations, the frequency of price changes varies significantly across goods, a pattern also documented by Nakamura and Steinsson (2008). Consistent with a positive average inflation rate in both panels, the average frequency of upward price changes exceeds that of the downward price changes in both cases.

A.2   Financial and Product-Market Firm Characteristics

We now describe the construction of firm-specific financial and product market indicators based on the quarterly Compustat data. In variable definitions, x_n denotes the Compustat data item n.

- **Cash and Short-Term Investments** (x_{30}): cash and all securities readily transferable to cash as listed in the current asset section of the firm's balance sheet.

- **Selling, General, and Administrative Expenses** (x_1): all commercial expenses of operation incurred in the regular course of business.

Table A-1: Summary Statistics of Good-Level Price Change Characteristics
(*Full PPI Sample vs. Matched PPI–Compustat Sample*)

Variable (percent)	Mean	SD	Min	P50	Max
Inflation					
Full PPI sample	0.15	0.82	−42.80	0.02	55.59
PPI–Compustat sample	0.12	0.57	−7.15	0.08	5.04
Positive price changes					
Full PPI sample	7.52	0.26	0.00	5.21	99.32
PPI–Compustat sample	6.21	6.19	0.00	4.80	89.45
Negative price changes					
Full PPI sample	−7.72	9.73	−99.88	−4.76	−0.00
PPI–Compustat sample	−6.70	8.39	−88.53	−4.38	−0.00
Freq. of price changes					
Full PPI sample	15.52	25.90	0.00	4.88	100.00
PPI–Compustat sample	18.31	27.28	0.00	6.90	100.00
Freq. of positive price changes					
Full PPI sample	9.14	14.45	0.00	3.45	100.00
PPI–Compustat sample	10.44	14.67	0.00	4.76	75.00
Freq. of negative price changes					
Full PPI sample	6.37	13.09	0.00	0.00	100.00
PPI–Compustat sample	7.87	13.68	0.00	1.52	100.00
Avg. number of goods per firm					
Full PPI sample	4.3	2.6	1	4	77
PPI–Compustat sample	5.4	3.3	1	4.9	41
Months in the panel					
Full PPI sample	42.3	25.3	1	41	96
PPI–Compustat sample	51.2	20.2	1	52	95

NOTE: Sample period: monthly data from Jan2005 to Dec2012. Full PPI sample: No. of goods = 202,281; No. of respondents = 46,306; and Obs. = 8,551,681. Matched PPI–Compustat sample: No. of goods = 6,859; No. of respondents = 1,242; and Obs. = 351,192. All price change characteristics correspond to good-level averages computed using trimmed monthly data.
SOURCES: Authors' calculations based on BLS PPI data and Compustat.

- **Net Sales** (x_2): gross sales (the amount of actual billings to customers for regular sales completed during the quarter) less cash discounts, trade discounts, returned sales, and allowances for which credit is given to customers.

- **Total Assets** (x_{44}): current assets plus net property, plant & equipment, plus other noncurrent assets.

The *liquidity ratio* is defined as the ratio of cash and short-term investments in quarter t to total assets in quarter t ($x_3[t]/x_{44}[t]$), and the *SGAX ratio* is defined as the ratio selling, general, and administrative expenses in quarter t to sales in quarter t ($x_1[t]/x_2[t]$). To ensure that our results were not influenced by a small number of extreme observations, we deleted from the quarterly Compustat panel data set all firm/quarter observations that failed to satisfy any of the following criteria:

1. $0.00 \leq$ Liquidity Ratio ≤ 1.00;

2. $0.00 \leq$ SGAX Ratio ≤ 10.0;

3. $-2.00 \leq \Delta \log(\text{Net Sales}) \leq 2.00$.

Table A-2: Summary Statistics for Selected Firm Characteristics
(U.S. Nonfinancial Corporate Sector vs. Matched PPI–Compustat Sample)

Variable	Mean	SD	Min	P50	Max
Sales ($bil.)[a]					
Compustat sample	0.96	4.44	$<$.01	0.08	200.41
PPI–Compustat sample	1.70	5.71	$<$.01	0.33	125.28
Liquidity ratio					
Compustat sample	0.21	0.24	0.00	0.12	1.00
PPI–Compustat sample	0.15	0.16	0.00	0.09	1.00
SGAX ratio					
Compustat sample	0.39	0.59	0.00	0.25	8.00
PPI–Compustat sample	0.26	0.29	0.00	0.21	7.77
Sales growth (pct.)					
Compustat sample	1.07	29.68	-199.97	1.65	199.94
PPI–Compustat sample	0.61	19.36	-197.12	1.32	176.49

NOTE: Sample period: Jan2005 to Dec2012 at a quarterly frequency. Compustat sample (U.S. nonfinancial sector): No. of firms = 6,138 and Obs. = 152,944. Matched PPI–Compustat sample: No. of firms = 584 and Obs. = 16,052. Liquidity ratio = cash & short-term investments to total assets; SGAX ratio = sales & general administrative expenses (SGAX) relative to sales. All statistics are based on trimmed data.
[a] Deflated by the U.S. nonfarm business sector GDP price deflator (2009:Q4 = 100).
SOURCES: Authors' calculations based on Compustat.

Table A-2 contains the selected summary statistics for the key variables used in the analysis for both the matched PPI–Compustat sample and for all U.S. nonfinancial firms covered by Compustat. In general, the PPI–Compustat sample contains larger firms—the median firm size, as measured by (quarterly) real sales, is more than $300 million, compared with only about $80 million for the entire Compustat sample. Reflecting their larger size, the firms in the PPI–Compustat panel tend to grow more slowly, on average, and also have less volatile sales. The difference in average firm size between the two data sets helps explain the fact that the aggregate dynamics of sales and prices of firms in the PPI–Compustat sample are representative of broader macroeconomic trends (see Figure 1).

In terms of financial characteristics, the two sets of firms are fairly similar, especially if one compares the respective medians of the two distributions. Nevertheless, firms in the PPI–Compustat sample tend to have somewhat less liquid balance sheets, on balance, as measured by the liquidity ratio. This difference is consistent with the fact that the PPI–Compustat sample consists of larger firms that, ceteris paribus, have better access to external sources of finance and therefore less need to maintain a precautionary liquidity buffer. An average firm in the PPI–Compustat sample also tends to have a lower SGAX ratio compared with an average nonfinancial firm in Compustat.

Figure A-1: Industry-Adjusted Producer Price Inflation
(*By Financial and Product-Market Characteristics and Durability of Output*)

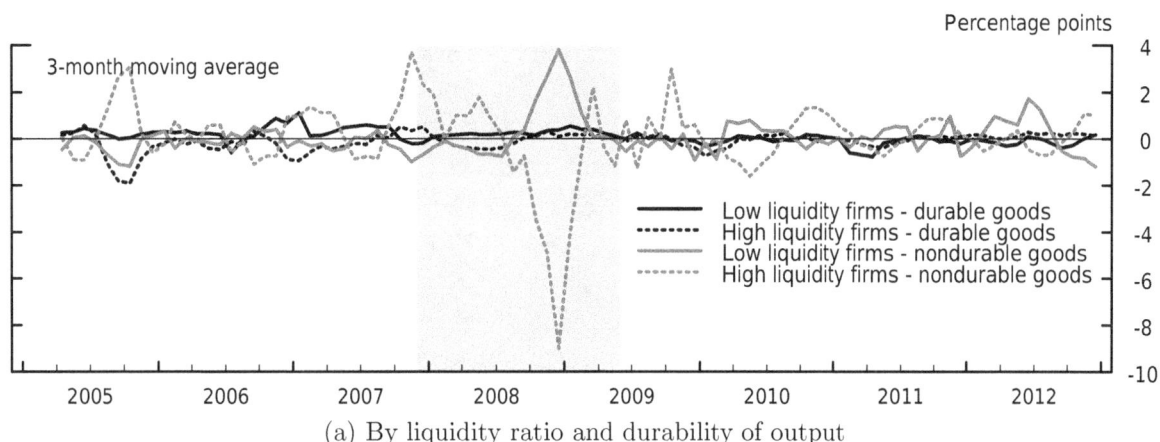

(a) By liquidity ratio and durability of output

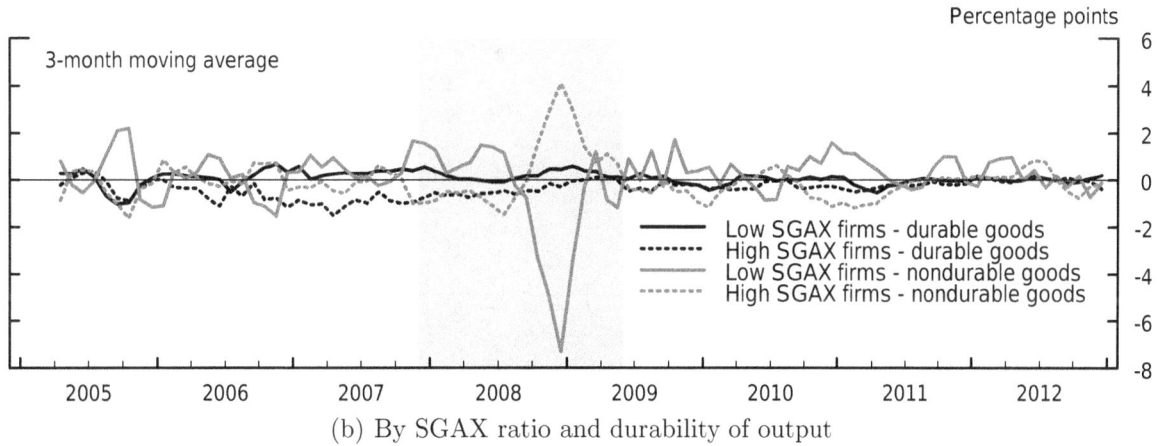

(b) By SGAX ratio and durability of output

NOTE: The solid (dotted) lines in panel (a) depicts the weighted-average industry-adjusted inflation rate for low (high) liquidity firms in durable and nondurable good manufacturing industries. The solid (dotted) lines in panel (b) depicts the weighted-average industry-adjusted inflation rate for low (high) SGAX firms in durable and nondurable good manufacturing industries. All series are seasonally adjusted. The shaded vertical bar represents the 2007–09 recession as dated by the NBER.
SOURCES: Authors' calculations based on BLS PPI data and Compustat.

A.3 Inflation Dynamics by Durability of Output

Panel (a) of Figure A-1 shows the industry-adjusted inflation rates of low and high liquidity firms within the durable and nondurable goods manufacturing sectors, while panel (b) displays the same information for firms with varying intensity of SG&A spending. This analysis is based on a subset of the matched PPI-Compustat data set, though, as noted in Section 2, more than 90 percent of goods in the matched PPI–Compustat data set are produced by manufacturing firms, split about evenly between durable and nondurable goods producers.

B Model Appendix

B.1 Model with Firm Heterogeneity and Nominal Rigidities

This section describes the key aspects of our full model—that is, the model featuring heterogeneous firms and nominal rigidities. Without loss of generality, we assume that there exist a finite number of firm types indexed by $k = 1, \ldots, N$. Firms of different types are characterized by varying degree of operating efficiency, measured by the size of the fixed operating cost. Formally, the production technology of firm i of type k is given by

$$y_{it} = \left(\frac{A_t}{a_{it}} h_{it} \right)^\alpha - \phi_k; \quad 0 < \alpha \le 1, \tag{B-1}$$

where $\phi_k \ge 0$ denotes the fixed operating costs, which can take one of N-values from a set $\boldsymbol{\Phi} = \{\phi_1, \ldots, \phi_N\}$, with $0 \le \phi_1 < \cdots < \phi_N$. The measure of firms of type k is denoted by Ξ_k, with $\sum_{k=1}^N \Xi_k = 1$. We assume that each type of firm faces the same distribution of the idiosyncratic productivity shock a_{it}—that is, $\log a_{it} \sim N(-0.5\sigma^2, \sigma^2)$, for all i and k.

The presence of quadratic adjustment costs incurred when firms change nominal prices modifies the flow-of-funds constraint as

$$0 = p_{it} c_{it} - w_t h_{it} - \frac{\gamma_p}{2} \left(\pi_t \frac{p_{it}}{p_{i,t-1}} - \bar{\pi} \right)^2 c_t - d_{it} + \varphi_t \min\{0, d_{it}\}. \tag{B-2}$$

The firm's problem of maximizing the expected present discounted value of dividends then gives rise to the following Lagrangian:

$$
\begin{aligned}
\mathcal{L} = \mathbb{E}_0 \sum_{t=0}^\infty m_{0,t} \Bigg\{ & d_{it} + \kappa_{it} \left[\left(\frac{A_t}{a_{it}} h_{it} \right)^\alpha - \phi_k - c_{it} \right] \\
& + \xi_{it} \left[p_{it} c_{it} - w_t h_{it} - \frac{\gamma_p}{2} \left(\pi_t \frac{p_{it}}{p_{i,t-1}} - \bar{\pi} \right)^2 c_t - d_{it} + \varphi_t \min\{0, d_{it}\} \right] \\
& + \nu_{it} \left[\left(\frac{p_{it}}{\tilde{p}_t} \right)^{-\eta} s_{it-1}^{\theta(1-\eta)} x_t - c_{it} \right] + \lambda_{it} \left[\rho s_{i,t-1} + (1-\rho) c_{it} - s_{it} \right] \Bigg\},
\end{aligned}
\tag{B-3}
$$

and the associated first-order conditions for type-k firms:

$$d_{it}: \quad \xi_{it} = \begin{cases} 1 & \text{if } d_{it} \ge 0 \\ 1/(1-\varphi_t) & \text{if } d_{it} < 0; \end{cases} \tag{B-4}$$

$$h_{it}: \quad \kappa_{it} = \xi_{it} a_{it} \left(\frac{w_t}{\alpha A_t} \right) (c_{it} + \phi_k)^{\frac{1-\alpha}{\alpha}}; \tag{B-5}$$

$$c_{it}: \quad \mathbb{E}_t^a[\nu_{it}] = \mathbb{E}_t^a[\xi_{it}] p_{it} - \mathbb{E}_t^a[\kappa_{it}] + (1-\rho) \mathbb{E}_t^a[\lambda_{it}]; \tag{B-6}$$

$$s_{it}: \quad \mathbb{E}_t^a[\lambda_{it}] = \rho \mathbb{E}_t^a[m_{t,t+1} \lambda_{i,t+1}] + \theta(1-\eta) \mathbb{E}_t \left[m_{t,t+1} \mathbb{E}_{t+1}^a[\nu_{i,t+1}] \left(\frac{c_{i,t+1}}{s_{it}} \right) \right]; \tag{B-7}$$

$$
\begin{aligned}
p_{it}: \quad 0 = & \, \mathbb{E}_t^a[\xi_{it}] c_{it} - \eta \frac{\mathbb{E}_t^a[\nu_{it}]}{p_{it}} c_{it} - \gamma_p \frac{\pi_t}{p_{i,t-1}} \left(\pi_t \frac{p_{it}}{p_{i,t-1}} - \bar{\pi} \right) c_t \\
& + \gamma_p \mathbb{E}_t \left[m_{t,t+1} \mathbb{E}_{t+1}^a[\xi_{i,t+1}] \pi_{t+1} \frac{p_{i,t+1}}{p_{it}^2} \left(\pi_{t+1} \frac{p_{i,t+1}}{p_{it}} - \bar{\pi} \right) c_{t+1} \right].
\end{aligned}
\tag{B-8}
$$

46

The presence of heterogeneous operating costs and nominal rigidities implies that the type-specific external financing trigger is given by

$$a_t^E(\phi_k) = \frac{c_{it}}{(c_{it} + \phi_k)^{\frac{1}{\alpha}}} \frac{A_t}{w_t} \left[p_{it} - \frac{\gamma_p}{2} \left(\pi_t \frac{p_{it}}{p_{i,t-1}} - \bar{\pi} \right)^2 \frac{c_t}{c_{it}} \right],$$ (B-9)

which allows us to express the first-order condition governing the behavior of dividends (equation B-4) as

$$\xi(a_{it}; \phi_k) = \begin{cases} 1 & \text{if } a_{it} \le a_t^E(\phi_k) \\ 1/(1 - \varphi_t) & \text{if } a_{it} > a_t^E(\phi_k). \end{cases}$$ (B-10)

Using equation (B-10), one can show that the expected shadow value of internal funds for firms of type k is equal to

$$\mathbb{E}_t^a[\xi_{it}|\phi_k] = \Phi(z_t^E(\phi_k)) + \frac{1}{1 - \varphi_t}\left[1 - \Phi(z_t^E(\phi_k))\right] = 1 + \frac{\varphi_t}{1 - \varphi_t}\left[1 - \Phi(z_t^E(\phi_k))\right] \ge 1,$$

where $z_t^E(\phi_k)$ denotes the standardized value of $a_t^E(\phi_k)$. Note that $da_t^E(\phi_k)/d\phi_k < 0$, which implies that $d\mathbb{E}_t^a[\xi_{it}|\phi_k]/d\phi_k > 0$. In other words, firms with lower operating efficiency are more likely to experience a liquidity shortfall and hence face a higher expected premium on external funds.

B.1.1 Aggregation

In the presence of firm heterogeneity, the nature of the symmetric equilibrium is modified. Specifically, all firms with the same ϕ_k choose the same price level P_{kt}:

$$P_{it}^{1-\eta} = \sum_{k=1}^N \mathbf{1}(\phi_i = \phi_k) \times P_{kt}^{1-\eta}.$$ (B-11)

Aggregate inflation dynamics are then given by a weighted average of the N types of firms. Because $\pi_t \equiv P_t/P_{t-1} = 1/P_{t-1}\left(\int_0^1 P_{it}^{1-\eta}di\right)^{1/(1-\eta)}$, we can use equation (B-11) to express the aggregate inflation rate as

$$\begin{aligned}
\pi_t &= \frac{1}{P_{t-1}}\left[\int_0^1 \sum_{k=1}^N \mathbf{1}(\phi_i = \phi_k) \times P_{kt}^{1-\eta}di\right]^{\frac{1}{1-\eta}} \\
&= \frac{1}{P_{t-1}}\left[\sum_{k=1}^N P_{kt}^{1-\eta}\int_0^1 \mathbf{1}(\phi_i = \phi_k)di\right]^{\frac{1}{1-\eta}} \\
&= \left[\sum_{k=1}^N \Xi_k \left(\frac{P_{kt}}{P_{t-1}}\right)^{1-\eta}\right]^{\frac{1}{1-\eta}} \\
&= \left[\sum_{k=1}^N \Xi_k \left(\frac{P_{kt}}{P_{k,t-1}}\right)^{1-\eta}\left(\frac{P_{k,t-1}}{P_{t-1}}\right)^{1-\eta}\right]^{\frac{1}{1-\eta}}.
\end{aligned}$$

Hence, the aggregate inflation rate is determined as a weighted-average of inflation rates of heterogeneous groups:

$$\pi_t = \left[\sum_{k=1}^N \Xi_k p_{k,t-1}^{1-\eta} \pi_{kt}^{1-\eta}\right]^{\frac{1}{1-\eta}},$$ (B-12)

where $\pi_{kt} \equiv P_{kt}/P_{k,t-1}$ is a type-specific inflation rate and $p_{kt} \equiv P_{kt}/P_t$ is a type-specific relative price. Note that the relative price p_{kt} can no longer be equalized to one in the symmetric equilibrium. The notion of a symmetric equilibrium is restricted to "within types," that is, within sectors, and in equilibrium, there exists a non-degenerate distribution of relative prices.

The following Phillips curve describes the inflation dynamics of the k-sector firms:

$$
\begin{aligned}
0 = p_{kt}\frac{c_{kt}}{c_t} &- \eta\frac{\mathbb{E}_t^a\left[\nu_{kit}|\phi_k\right]}{\mathbb{E}_t^a\left[\xi_{kit}|\phi_k\right]}\frac{c_{kt}}{c_t} - \gamma_p\pi_{kt}\pi_t\left(\pi_{kt}\pi_t - \bar{\pi}\right) \\
&+ \gamma_p\mathbb{E}_t\left[m_{t,t+1}\frac{\mathbb{E}_{t+1}^a\left[\xi_{ki,t+1}|\phi_k\right]}{\mathbb{E}_t^a\left[\xi_{kit}|\phi_k\right]}\pi_{k,t+1}\pi_{t+1}\left(\pi_{k,t+1}\pi_{t+1} - \bar{\pi}\right)\frac{c_{t+1}}{c_t}\right].
\end{aligned}
\tag{B-13}
$$

The same notion of the modified symmetric equilibrium can be applied to equilibrium output:

$$
c_{it}^j = \sum_{k=1}^N \mathbf{1}(\phi_i = \phi_k) \times c_{kt}^j.
$$

Because the household sector is still characterized by a symmetric equilibrium, we can drop the "j" superscript. The individual demand for products produced by firms with efficiency rank k is then given by

$$
c_{kt} = \left(\frac{p_{kt}}{\tilde{p}_t}\right)^{-\eta} s_{k,t-1}^{\theta(1-\eta)} x_t,
\tag{B-14}
$$

where

$$
\tilde{p}_t = \left[\sum_{k=1}^N \Xi_k p_{kt}^{1-\eta} s_{k,t-1}^{\theta(1-\eta)}\right]^{\frac{1}{1-\eta}};
\tag{B-15}
$$

and

$$
x_t = \left[\sum_{k=1}^N \Xi_k\left(\frac{c_{kt}}{s_{k,t-1}^\theta}\right)^{1-\frac{1}{\eta}}\right]^{\frac{1}{1-\frac{1}{\eta}}}.
\tag{B-16}
$$

Aggregate demand should then satisfy

$$
c_t = \left[\sum_{k=1}^N \Xi_k\left[\exp(0.5\alpha(1+\alpha)\sigma^2)h_{kt}^\alpha - \phi_k\right]^{1-\frac{1}{\eta}}\right]^{\frac{1}{1-\frac{1}{\eta}}},
\tag{B-17}
$$

while the type-specific conditional labor demand satisfies

$$
h_{kt} = \left[\frac{c_{kt} + \phi_k}{\exp(0.5\alpha(1+\alpha)\sigma^2)}\right]^{\frac{1}{\alpha}},
\tag{B-18}
$$

with $h_t = \sum_{k=1}^N h_{kt}$. (The term $\exp(0.5\alpha(1+\alpha)\sigma^2)$ is the expected value of $1/a_{it}$, which is strictly greater than one due to Jensen's inequality.)

B.1.2 Equilibrium Relative Prices in the Steady State

In the steady state, the Phillips curve (equation B-13) implies

$$
p_k = \eta\frac{\mathbb{E}^a\left[\nu_i|\phi_k\right]}{\mathbb{E}^a\left[\xi_i|\phi_k\right]}.
\tag{B-19}
$$

48

From the first-order conditions for the habit stock (equation B-7), we have

$$\frac{\mathbb{E}^a\big[\lambda_i|\phi_k\big]}{\mathbb{E}^a\big[\xi_i|\phi_k\big]} = \frac{\theta(1-\eta)\beta}{1-\rho\beta}\frac{\mathbb{E}^a\big[\nu_i|\phi_k\big]}{\mathbb{E}^a\big[\xi_i|\phi_k\big]}. \tag{B-20}$$

Combining equations (B-19) and (B-20) yields

$$\frac{\mathbb{E}^a\big[\lambda_i|\phi_k\big]}{\mathbb{E}^a\big[\xi_i|\phi_k\big]} = p_k\frac{\theta(1-\eta)\beta}{\eta(1-\rho\beta)}. \tag{B-21}$$

In the steady state, the first-order conditions for labor input (equation B-5) and production scale (equation B-6) together imply

$$\frac{\mathbb{E}^a\big[\nu_i|\phi_k\big]}{\mathbb{E}^a\big[\xi_i|\phi_k\big]} = -\frac{\mathbb{E}^a\big[\xi_i a_i|\phi_k\big]}{\mathbb{E}^a\big[\xi_i|\phi_k\big]}\frac{w}{\alpha A}\left(c_k+\phi_k\right)^{\frac{1-\alpha}{\alpha}}+p_k+(1-\rho)\frac{\mathbb{E}^a\big[\lambda_i|\phi_k\big]}{\mathbb{E}^a\big[\xi_i|\phi_k\big]}. \tag{B-22}$$

Substituting equations (B-19) and (B-21) into equation (B-22) yields

$$p_k = \frac{\eta(1-\rho\beta)}{(\eta-1)[(1-\rho\beta)-\theta\beta(1-\rho)]}\frac{\mathbb{E}^a\big[\xi_i a_i|\phi_k\big]}{\mathbb{E}^a\big[\xi_i|\phi_k\big]}\frac{w}{\alpha A}\left(c_k+\phi_k\right)^{\frac{1-\alpha}{\alpha}}. \tag{B-23}$$

The sector-specific external financing triggers in the steady state are given by

$$a_k^E = \frac{p_k c_k}{(c_k+\phi_k)^{\frac{1}{\alpha}}}\frac{A}{w}, \tag{B-24}$$

while the consumption aggregators imply

$$\frac{c_k}{c_l} = \left(\frac{p_k}{p_l}\right)^{-\eta}\frac{s_k^{\theta(1-\eta)}}{s_l^{\theta(1-\eta)}}; \quad k\neq l, \tag{B-25}$$

and

$$x = \left[\sum_{k=1}^{N}\Xi_k\left(c_k^{1-\theta}\right)^{1-\frac{1}{\eta}}\right]^{\frac{1}{1-\frac{1}{\eta}}}. \tag{B-26}$$

General equilibrium consistency conditions require

$$1 = \left[\sum_{k=1}^{N}\Xi_k p_k^{1-\eta}\right]^{\frac{1}{1-\eta}}, \tag{B-27}$$

which is the steady-state version of equation (B-12), with $\pi = \pi_k = 1$.

The household j's preferences over the habit-adjusted consumption bundle x_t^j and labor h_t^j are given by the following (CRRA) utility function:

$$U(x_t^j, h_t^j) = \frac{x_t^{1-\theta_x}}{1-\theta_x} - \frac{\zeta}{1+\theta_h}h_t^{1+\theta_h}.$$

The resulting market-clearing conditions associated with the labor and goods markets imply

$$\frac{w}{\tilde{p}}x^{-\theta_x} = \zeta h^{\theta_h}, \tag{B-28}$$

49

and

$$c = \left[\sum_{k=1}^{N} \Xi_k \left[\exp(0.5\alpha(1+\alpha)\sigma^2)h_k^\alpha - \phi_k \right]^{1-\frac{1}{\eta}} \right]^{\frac{1}{1-\frac{1}{\eta}}}, \tag{B-29}$$

respectively, where the sector-specific conditional labor demand satisfies

$$h_k = \left[\frac{c_k + \phi_k}{\exp(0.5\alpha(1+\alpha)\sigma^2)} \right]^{\frac{1}{\alpha}}, \tag{B-30}$$

with

$$h = \sum_{k=1}^{N} h_k. \tag{B-31}$$

In the steady state, the deep-habit adjusted price index is given by

$$\tilde{p} = \left[\sum_{k=1}^{N} \Xi_k p_k^{1-\eta} c_k^{\theta(1-\eta)} \right]^{\frac{1}{1-\eta}}, \tag{B-32}$$

which is the steady-state version of equation (B-15). The system of equations (B-23)–(B-32) can then be solved numerically for $4N + 5$ variables: p_k, c_k, a_k^E, and h_k, $k = 1, \ldots, N$; and x, w, $\tilde{p}$, h, and c.

B.2   The Log-Linearized Phillips Curve

To derive the log-linearized Phillips curve (equation 26 in the main text), we use the first-order condition with respect to p_{it} (equation B-8), impose the symmetric equilibrium conditions (that is, $p_{it} = 1$ and $c_{it} = c_t$), and log-linearize the resulting expression to obtain

$$\hat{\pi}_t = -\frac{1}{\gamma_p}(\hat{\nu}_t - \hat{\xi}_t) + \beta\mathbb{E}_t\left[\hat{\pi}_{t+1}\right], \tag{B-33}$$

where $\hat{x}_t$ denotes the log-deviation of a generic variable x_t from its deterministic steady-state value of $\bar{x}$. In equation (B-33), the term $\hat{\nu}_t - \hat{\xi}_t$ is the log-deviation of the ratio $\mathbb{E}_t^a[\nu_{it}]/\mathbb{E}_t^a[\xi_{it}]$, which measures the value of internal funds relative to that of marginal sales:

$$\frac{\mathbb{E}_t^a[\nu_{it}]}{\mathbb{E}_t^a[\xi_{it}]} = 1 - \frac{\mathbb{E}_t^a[\kappa_{it}]}{\mathbb{E}_t^a[\xi_{it}]} + (1-\rho)\frac{\mathbb{E}_t^a[\lambda_{it}]}{\mathbb{E}_t^a[\xi_{it}]}. \tag{B-34}$$

Using the first-order condition with respect to h_{it} (equation B-5), one can show that the first two terms on the right-hand side of equation (B-34) are equivalent to $(\tilde{\mu}_t - 1)/\tilde{\mu}_t$, where $\tilde{\mu}_t \equiv \mu_t\mathbb{E}_t^a[\xi_{it}]/\mathbb{E}_t^a[\xi_{it}a_{it}]$ is the financially adjusted markup. By iterating the first-order condition with respect to the habit stock s_{it} forward, the closed-form solution for the last term in equation (B-34) is given by

$$\frac{\mathbb{E}_t^a[\lambda_{it}]}{\mathbb{E}_t^a[\xi_{it}]} = \theta(1-\eta)\mathbb{E}_t\left[\sum_{s=t}^{\infty} \tilde{\beta}_{t,s+1} \frac{\mathbb{E}_s^a[\xi_{i,s+1}]}{\mathbb{E}_t^a[\xi_{it}]} \left(\frac{\tilde{\mu}_{s+1}-1}{\tilde{\mu}_{s+1}} \right) \right], \tag{B-35}$$

where

$$\tilde{\beta}_{t,s+1} \equiv m_{s,s+1}g_{s+1} \times \prod_{j=1}^{s-t} [\rho + \theta(1-\eta)(1-\rho)g_{t+j}]m_{t+j-1,t+j}$$

denotes the growth-adjusted discount factor and $g_t \equiv c_t/s_{t-1} = (s_t/s_{t-1} - \rho)/(1 - \rho)$.

To obtain the term $\hat{\nu}_t - \hat{\xi}_t$ in equation (B-33), we substitute equation (B-35) into equation (B-34) and log-linearize the right-hand side of the resulting expression. The log-linearized Phillips curve can then be expressed as

$$
\begin{aligned}
\hat{\pi}_t &= -\frac{\omega(\eta - 1)}{\gamma}\left[\hat{\mu}_t + \mathbb{E}_t \sum_{s=t}^{\infty} \chi\tilde{\delta}^{s-t+1}\hat{\mu}_{s+1}\right] + \beta\mathbb{E}_t\left[\hat{\pi}_{t+1}\right] \\
&\quad + \frac{1}{\gamma}\left[\eta - \omega(\eta - 1)\right]\mathbb{E}_t \sum_{s=t}^{\infty} \chi\tilde{\delta}^{s-t+1}\left[(\hat{\xi}_t - \hat{\xi}_{s+1}) - \hat{\beta}_{t,s+1}\right],
\end{aligned}
$$

where $\omega = 1 - \beta\theta(1 - \rho)/(1 - \rho\beta)$ and $\tilde{\delta} = \beta[\rho + \theta(1 - \eta)(1 - \rho)]$.